THE IDEALS OF FREEDOM

Challenging Contemporary Misconceptions

MEZIE OKOLO

THE IDEALS OF FREEDOM:

Challenging Contemporary Misconceptions

mezieokolo@gmail.com

ISBN-10: 099058030X

ISBN-13: 978-0-9905803-0-0

PRINTED IN THE UNITED STATES OF AMERICA

To the loving memory of all heroes of freedom

Acknowledgments

Over the years, I have benefited from the grace and mercies of God. I have also learnt that unless the Lord builds the house, in vain do the builders sweat in labor and waste man-hour. There is no such thing as a self-made man. Such thoughts come from the idle mind of a proud man of ingratitude.

Some of my associates at Fort Stockton discussed this topic as I developed the arguments, especially Amalia Flores and Ann Ricciardi. A couple of my friends also answered my question: What does freedom mean to you? For taking the time to respond to that post, you are appreciated: Dr. Joshua Madumere (UK), Uzoma Ezeike (UK), Paschal Igbena (UK), Joy Onyemelukwe (USA), Charles Igbokwe (USA), Dr Dani Ogo Nsofor (USA), Goodluck Nwadike (Nigeria), Peace N Chineke (Nigeria), Bibbi Ofoje (Nigeria), Ejike Iwuogaranya (USA), Evans Ngozi Onwu (Nigeria), Dr. Elias E. Elemike (Nigeria) and Dr. Adekunle Rowaiye (Nigeria).

Others are Kim K Falcon (USA), Jonas Nweke (USA), Obianuju Umunna (Nigeria), Density Sunday Abraham (UK), Kenneth Ibeanusi (Nigeria), Dr. Godwin Ude (Canada), Peter Agu (Nigeria), Evanson Sambala (UK), Amaka O Okoro (Nigeria), Damian Odumegwu (Germany), Silas Evumude (Nigeria), Ijeoma Onyemesili (UK), Ukamaka Nkwuaku-Ikechukwu (Nigeria), Martin Agility Agbili (Nigeria) and Johnson Awa (Nigeria).

Worthy of thanks are my friends Jodie Bailey Day, Jamie Batson, Constantine Chibundu, Dr. Pascal Onyema, Vincent Egwuonwu, Dr. Fred Anigwe, Eddie Abikhui and Elder Uzo Uzoma. My gratitude also goes to all who have supported me in one way or the other in my struggle for freedom, especially Ngozi and Dr Forster E Samuel-Ihejiofor, Chief Sam C Uka, Festus C Obi, Prof. P Nwachukwu Okpala, Pastor Isaac Aladeniyi, Chinyere Okam, Grace and Sonny Obuseh, Maria and Uzo Anaele, Prof. Charles Esimone, Prof. Chuck Arize and Dr Yele Aluko.

My love to my siblings Chinyere, Chimara, Chidi, Nonye, Nchedo, Rev. Ekene, Chioma and Ikem; for the memories of growing up together in the little town of Ogbunka, back in the day. My parents Janet and Apollos Okolo are still doing very well taking care of the home front while the rest of us have scattered to the four corners of the earth.

My wife, Chidimma Okolo and my two lovely daughters, Chisom and Udodi are the best. You all have supported my quest to put in writing the ideas that flow through my mind. Intellectual activity is done more efficiently in a peaceful and tranquil environment.

All lovers of freedom, and those who have dedicated their lives fighting for it are hereby celebrated. As we struggle, let us not forget that freedom is an ideal that is attained through ordeals. Keep up the good work…"a luta continua, victoria e certa!"

PREFACE

There exists such a huge difference between what we think freedom should be and what it actually is. For example, physical incarceration may but does not always lead to mental incapacitation. Incarcerated mind begets incapacitated hands. There are too many people roaming the streets whose minds are incarcerated…those are in need of freedom, urgently. Therefore freedom can be viewed as the absence, not of fettered hands but of fettered minds.

In an opinion poll aimed at knowing what freedom means to my friends, some of the participants have these to say about freedom:

- Freedom is the ability to overcome
- Freedom is actualized the moment a set goal is achieved
- You have freedom when you are in Christ, because you are no longer slave to anybody or thing
- Freedom makes man equal to God
- Absolute freedom is not sold in the open market, it can only be bought in Christ
- There is an unconscious restriction beneath every freedom

- We achieve greater freedom when we work more in group not as individuals
- Freedom is about self belief…knowledge frees the spirit and you cannot enslave the enlightened mind. That is the essence of freedom

Sometimes, the restrictive nature of freedom undermines the very essence of it and in fact makes it seem like a mere idea, a dream, a wish that may never materialize. It has eluded many even in supposedly free societies.

Freedom begins with knowledge. Ignorance leads to bondage while knowledge leads to freedom. However, knowledge is necessary but not sufficient for freedom to become a reality. Even then, the freedom so attained is still restrictive. This is because, while you express yourself in freedom for example, you are still conscious of the boundaries. There is freedom in knowing where the boundaries are and respecting them.

As we figure out what freedom is, I know it is not making your own rules; rather it is being law-abiding and obeying the rules, both written and unwritten. Everybody is a slave to someone or something. Although man has the potential to make choices, many do not have the power to make and stick to the choice they want to make. For example, why is it such a challenge to stop a habit like smoking?

It is one thing to have the power and ability to do something; it is another thing to have the will to do it.

Without the will, power is disabled; and without power, the will is incapacitated.

In the end, we suggest that the following explain our freedom as Christians

- Jesus bought freedom for us. Freedom is never given freely
- He said to us "Take my yoke upon you and learn of me". Either way, there is a yoke to bear.
- God set the Israelites free in Egypt but the scripture is full of rules, commandments and restrictions He gave them.
- The freedom that Jesus secures translates us from slaves of sin/the devil to slaves of God. It sounds like a paradox, but Paul the apostle admonishes Christians to live like slaves of God.
- With freedom, He gave us power: freedom to be...and power (not necessarily, freedom) to do ... The questions are, "freedom to be what and power to do what?" What does freedom mean to you as an individual? Are you free? Free from what? Free to be what? Free to do what?

These are some of the questions we will answer in the pages that follow. Stay with us and we will make this journey to the world of freedom, together.

TABLE OF CONTENTS

INTRODUCTION

There are probably as many definitions of freedom as there are people who have tried to define it. Growing up in eastern Nigeria, I recall a lot of noise, songs, jingles and cartoons about the struggles for freedom, either of apartheid in South Africa, the Biafran attempt at independence, the anti-racism movements in the United States, the agitations from the Ogoni people of Nigeria and the movements for liberation in Liberia, Namibia and several other emancipation campaigns. Each of these and related struggles was peculiar, yet remarkable. They all share a common theme: to liberate a nation and her people from the tyranny of another.

Everywhere in the world somebody feels a need for freedom – from an oppressive boss, an abusive husband, a tyrannical leader of a sort, or from false brethren who look for opportunities everywhere and every time to take advantage of the relatively gullible and disadvantaged. Those who are in positions of authority and power tend to forget that we hold this truth to be self evident, that all men were born equal, regardless of their tribe, genealogy, creed, skin color, accent and the like.

In most of Africa for example, nation states were struggling for freedom mainly in the form of Independence, as far back as the 1940s. In Social Studies classes, we learnt a lot about those struggles for independence and such movements as Zikism. Until I lived in England among people of diverse backgrounds and mindsets, I did not fully appreciate the gallantry exhibited by the people who fought for and got independence for all the countries previously ruled by the colonial masters. It is not easy to go to the house of a strong man and set his captives free. Otherwise, Jesus should not have died so that we may live. The cost of freedom is too much for most people who clamor for, sometime, the freedom they neither understand nor can they define. As soon as some can estimate the real cost, most people draw back and give up, change the music or the dancing steps. Most times, it takes the anointed and motivated to stand the heat.

Think about the United States and her fight for independence prior to 1795. The men who signed the documents to declare independence understood what they were up against and what punishment they risked. It was a treasonable felony to sign such a document which was a direct indictment on the King of England. The men were bold, meant business but risked annihilation. One of them, who had a form of shaky-hand disorder, was quoted to have said "my hands shake but my heart does not shake". Another one wrote his name in bolds and when asked he said "so that the King of England could read it without his spectacles". It takes courage to do that.

In the pursuit of freedom, people risk losing the freedom they already enjoy, howbeit momentarily. A story of the Israelites in Egypt readily comes to mind. They had been in bondage and knew not how else to live life but that of bondage. After over four hundred years, whatever the life they lived had become norm. They were accustomed with slavery, and could not even aspire to independence anymore. They were hewing wood, fetching water, doing janitorial jobs and making bricks. Their generations had done the same thing that it was unimaginable talking to anybody about freedom.

Even the slave masters were used to having their menial jobs and chores done by these Hebrews that thinking otherwise was like imagining the suicidal. Don't forget that Egypt had a very organized and impeccable system under Pharaoh. As a matter of fact, we are told that civilization started in Egypt. Their army was probably second to none at that time. If the Israelites sized them up, any thoughts of freedom would turn to nightmares. You don't set your battle in array with an enemy who has machine guns, when all you have is a catapult, unless your name is David and the enemy Goliath of Gath.

From nowhere Moses shows up with a claim of deliverance message from Yahweh, who introduced himself as "I am". Have you ever expected good news from a venture, only to experience nothing but disaster? Is that not why many people are in bondage because they are afraid to trouble the waters not knowing if they can predict, let alone survive the consequences? Any action taken to secure freedom for somebody comes with serious consequences.

As Moses introduced a topic everybody wanted but nobody was courageous enough to even imagine, it was not very difficult to get the Israelites on board especially after he had demonstrated the wonders and miracles, even though he had never been a magician. However, that did not rule out the fear of the people about stepping on toes. Pharaoh was as powerful in those days as Caesar of Rome, or probably the King of England in the days when the declaration of independence for the United States was signed. Every time the subject of freedom is introduced to a discussion or brought up in the agenda or contract, one risks stepping on toes and being adequately punished for it. We shall explore that in more detail shortly.

As anybody would have expected, freedom always comes at a great price…oh yes, mere introduction of the topic in settings is frowned at. Pharaoh called them lazy and considered them idle, so had to increase their burdens. If you molded one hundred bricks when somebody else provided the straws, now you have to go fetch your straws and still mold the same number of bricks. That is mean and the approach draconian. What did you expect of the people? They murmured. If we organized a murmuring competition, I bet Israelites would win. The people wanted freedom but not the inconveniences of attaining it. The mere fact that they murmured means that they did not have the freedom of speech that we abuse today.

If we conduct a survey, you would be amazed how people think God should orchestrate their deliverance and secure their freedom, but God's ways are different from ours. Before He sent Moses, he had already planned the deliverance, and appropriately budgeted for it. Unknown to Moses, God had drawn up His agenda for Pharaoh and Egypt and would not stop until He had played the script fully. As a result, He hardened the heart of Pharaoh, so that both Egyptians and Israelites would fear Him.

When you see miracles first hand, you have to believe or someone will believe for you. The kingdom of God does not consist in words and too much grammar, but in the demonstration of power. As soon as power meets power, the stronger one swallows the weaker just like Moses' snake swallowed the snakes of the magicians of Egypt. That is called "Power Pass Power". By the time men thought that God had finished in Egypt, God was still not satisfied...He wanted Pharaoh and his men to perish also. So He caused them to pursue after Israel.

Leaving Egypt was a great deliverance but drowning Pharaoh and his men was a greater deliverance. Did you see that the women were singing and dancing "Sing unto the Lord for He has triumphed gloriously, the horse and its riders He has thrown into the sea"? There was no doubt in the mind of anyone that only God could have done what they just witnessed with their own eyes. It had never been imagined, nor had it been told in history that any such mighty acts had been done. I can imagine all Israel dancing joyfully and celebrating their freedom lavishly, everyman in his own ways. God inhabits the praises of his people.

CHAPTER 1

IN THE PURSUIT OF FREEDOM

The whole world is in need of freedom. The subject of freedom is much talked about but certainly not as much understood. It appears simple and straightforward until you sit down to think about it in tangible, measurable terms. The big question is "what is freedom?" That is more difficult to answer than "what does freedom mean to you?' The later has no right or wrong answer so anybody is welcome to say anything that makes sense to him given his situation, or life experiences.

When you consider the former, "what is freedom?" then you realize that what freedom means to many of us has no bearing to what freedom actually is. Does it then mean that we are looking for what we don't know? How then can we recognize it when we find it? Alternatively, is freedom a means to an end and not an end in itself? That is, do you need freedom so you can do something or be something OR do you need freedom for the sake of freedom?

For intellectual exercise, anybody can choose to travel in either direction. We would leave the debates and arguments for the philosophers. For the purposes of this book, we will look at freedom in three dimensions

- Freedom from
- Freedom to be
- Freedom to do

Freedom FROM...oppression, subjugation, slavery, apartheid, abuse, fear, addiction, harassment, debt, lack, want, agony, manipulation, suppression, hunger, despondency, bureaucracy, discrimination, racism, sexism, tribalism etc

Freedom to BE...

- Self determined: Decide who you are and be left alone for who you want to be.
- Freedom to be respected for who and what you are or what you have attained: a human being; a citizen of a country; a professional in your own field; a head of household
- Freedom to pursue your dreams and become what you want to be without overt or covert institutionalized discriminatory restrictions or practices (schools for the poor only, hospitals for colored people, buses for straight people, pubs for white only, military recruitment for local college graduates only)

Freedom to DO...

- Political freedom: to vote and be voted for

- Freedom of speech: to freely express yourself
- Religious freedom: to choose for yourself who you will serve, "but as for me and my household, there is no voting: we will serve the Lord".
- Freedom to engage in an economic activity of your choice: get loans to start a business and compete on a level ground without facing more huddles than anyone else.

****

A few questions that come to mind while talking about freedom are

- Are the constitutions of countries of the world color blind and are they enforced color-blinded? If not, why does it seem like some people get away with things others would not?
- Slaves and slave masters are dead and gone from our midst, but is slavery still here with us in our market places, schools, churches etc OR do people still live with slave and/or slave master mentalities?
- We don't have any places marked as "for tall people" or "for red people" but when you go to some neighborhoods, all short people move out if any tall person moves in. On a Sunday morning, we know to sit at home and watch television than to walk into the church next door and worship with people that don't look like us. How free is the society, the church and the community?

It is said that everything that has advantage also has disadvantages, right? We all believe that freedom has advantages. What are the disadvantages of freedom? Let us look at a few examples. We all like to eat, and eating has advantages, right? What are the disadvantages of eating? Somebody said that one of the disadvantages is that you have to visit the rest room. Ok, I agree. Most of us want to go to heaven, because we think it has advantages. What are the disadvantages of that? You have to first die before you go to heaven. You miss your friends, family and colleagues who are still alive and on earth. Nobody wants to die, right? What are the advantages of death? You go to heaven. Also, you become free from all the cares and worries and fears of life – no bills to pay, no mortgages, no student loans, no credit cards to service, no car notes, etc. That is a long list of the things we want to be free from, yet we don't want to die. Why? I thought we all want and need freedom?

If you don't know what you are looking for, you will definitely not know when you find it. His middle name was Nwaama – a young teenage boy who recently graduated from a village high school in the days before cell phones became readily available to every Tom, Dick and Harry. Soon after, he went to stay with his uncle in the city. Being a smart boy, within weeks he began to drive and was actually very confident, even though he had no driver's license.

His uncle traveled out of town. The uncle's driver was sick, so did not come to work. His uncle's friend was flying into town from overseas. Nwaama had never met the uncle's friend but volunteered to go pick him up at the airport…with the zeal of a new but unlicensed driver. The office manager described how he would go, and some of the relevant vital information but apparently, Nwaama did not understand, yet he claimed he did. Off to the airport he zoomed.

But Nwaama was raised by his dad who was a very mean ex-military officer. Nwaama's dad had an old 404 Peugeot Saloon that Nwaama was never allowed to even crank the engine, let alone drive the car, but he was mandated to make sure to wash the car every morning. For him, freedom means being allowed to "warm" or drive a car, especially after it is washed. He couldn't wait to graduate, so he could leave his father's house in search of freedom. It was another instance of zeal without knowledge – common among present day teenagers.

Men and women, boys and girls, black and white, chiefs and Indians all trooped in and out of the airport as one plane after the other arrived at the terminals. Nwaama was obviously carried away by the scenes. He was having fun, cracking jokes with standers-by and enjoying the moment. He forgot the carrier he was waiting for, and the plane Josh boarded. He didn't know when Josh arrived. He recalled seeing this man looking around, searching for somebody in the multitude but he had no inkling that was the man he came to pick up. Those were not the days when everybody has cell phones, and for crying out loud, Nwaama was new in the city- he just came the other day.

As soon as Josh got to Nwaama's uncle Jim's house in a cab, they began to look for Nwaama. Where has he gone to? Did he make it to the airport? Did he get involved in a wreck? Have the police men arrested him, probably for traffic offences? Maybe the area boys got him? Does he even have a drivers' license? Hope he did not scratch somebody's car and got into trouble? Why did Lucy let him go to the airport by himself; somebody should have gone with him?

They sent the cab driver to go look for him. Nwaama's dad, who had come into town earlier in the day, volunteered to go with the taxi driver even though he is not too familiar with the road network and the airport. They searched for him all over the places, asking people with a description of how he looked, to see if they saw anybody that met those descriptions. Eventually they saw him sitting at one corner, talking and joking with a school mate of his, Joke. She had come to the airport with her aunty to pick up her uncle who was flying in from Dubai.

It was like a dream, no, a joke. From nowhere what he heard was Nwa ama ihe o na-acho. Before he could answer, Chief Ekwueme slapped him on his cheek, and stars fell off his eyes. He bent over, and covered his face with his two palms. He wanted to cry, but wouldn't cry in the presence of a girl, else he would communicate that he is not man enough. He wished he could slap back, but then standers-by would beat him up the African way for fighting his dad in the public. He was not even sure if that was a dream, an apparition, or reality, because he had no idea his dad was in Lagos, let alone at the airport. His hands and legs wobbled, as he sobbed and couldn't drive. Chief took over the driving; it was the longest journey Nwaama had made in his entire life. Those thirty minutes of driving back to the uncle's house seemed like thirty years.

Eventually they got to uncle Jim's house in Adekunle Village. Nwaama was still sobbing and sorrowful. He was still confused. What was his dad doing in the city? When did he come? Why did he slap him in the presence of a girl? He thought his father would take him back to Umuchim. He was yet to celebrate freedom from his dad when he left the village, only to be embarrassed in the city.

At Uncle Jim's house, Josh came and was consoling him. He had never seen Josh – a whitish man who he saw at the airport without recognizing him as the one he actually came to pick up. At that time, Josh had been rested for several hours. Nobody could explain to Nwaama why everybody was mad with him, and he did not understand it either. He thought he gained freedom the day he left his father's house for Lagos, now he realizes it still eludes him; moreover he didn't think it was a big deal that he did not see Josh at the airport, and did not know he had gone by the cab. If he could have come by the cab, why did they send him in the first place?

CHAPTER 2

THE GENESIS OF FREEDOM

"You may freely eat fruit from every tree of the orchard, but you must not eat from the tree of the knowledge of good and evil" (Gen. 2:16-17). This is the very first account of the mention of freedom in scriptures. As we see from the creation accounts (Gen.1&2), after Adam was formed from the dust of the earth, God knew that the man needed to be gainfully employed. His original job was to be a gardener - to tend the orchard which the Lord had planted in Eden. These trees/plants did not grow by natural means because rain had not even fallen on the face of the earth. Before the idea to create Eve was conceived, Adam had his first commandment which incorporated the word "free". God created man to exercise some form of freedom in his environment.

Think about it. Man was formed, and the orchard was planted for man. God even made all kinds of trees grow from the soil and these were not thorns and thistles, but trees that were pleasing to look at and good for food. But in the middle were two trees as noted earlier (Gen. 2:9).

God made river to flow from Eden to water the garden. There was pure gold, pearls and precious stones also provided to decorate the garden for Adam's enjoyment. God placed Adam in the orchard in Eden to care for it and to maintain it. You know that the laborer is worthy of the first fruit. Freely eat of all but these two in the center. As soon as that commandment was given to Adam in clear languages, the next agenda was to create Eve (verse 18). So the commandment not to eat from the tree at the center of the garden pre-dated Eve. Apparently, Adam had told Eve what God said, as they played around and had fun in the beautiful garden designed by God himself. Nowadays we have all kinds of gardens and parks, but none is anything to be compared with the very first garden not planted by human hands.

The man God created enjoyed freedom in the garden God had designed for him...but it was not absolute freedom. There were more than enough plants in the garden, good to behold and good for food, but man abused the very first freedom he had, by exercising yet another freedom- the freedom of choice, to which we will return shortly.

Every time we forget the extent of our freedom, we err. Every act of disobedience has consequences no matter how mild or remediable. God created all the living things, man named them. Whatever Adam called anything, that is its name till this day. That was creative as well.

At Eden, Adam exercised and enjoyed the freedom of innovative nomenclature and creative taxonomy. He had the power and ability to discern by the Spirit of God in him. As soon as he saw Eve, he recognized her as the bone of his bone and the flesh of his flesh even though he was asleep when his rib bone was taken. He even called her "woman"…can you see creative taxonomy? It was life as God intended it.

THE TEMPTER COMES

The talking serpent shows up to chat with Eve. Adam was probably at one corner tending the orchard, and plucking flowers for his wife. They were in their place of assignment and probably discharging their duties when the tempter came. You do not have to be delinquent from your place of assignment for him to show up, he comes in right where God has planted you, and he aims to stop you from blossoming. The serpent begins to question God's word and instruction that was a standing order before Eve was created.

"Is it really true that God said, you must not eat any tree of the orchard? No, that's not what God said, because Eve knew what God said (Gen 3:1). Your knowledge of what God said in His word is good, but not sufficient to deliver you on the day of evil; your obedience to the Word is what guarantees safety and freedom. "We may eat of the fruit from the trees of the orchard (vs. 2) but the tree in the middle". The serpent went ahead to inform the woman that God was a "liar". "Surely you will not die" (Gen 3:4); for God does not want your eyes to be open so you don't become divine beings, knowing good and evil (vs 5). Eve examined the tree more closely. It was good for food (like other trees), attractive to the eye (like others in the orchard) and desirable for making one wise. How did she know it was desirable for making one wise? Why did she need any extra wisdom? Was the need for wisdom her problem in Eden? Was she ambitious of becoming "divine being'?

If anyone lacks wisdom, let him ask God who gives liberally. Nobody becomes wise by disobedience; neither does anybody become wise by adhering to the counsel of a talking serpent, or fellowshipping with him. There are too many talking serpents going around, with false doctrines of "freedom". Apparently, the mission of the serpent was to talk man into disobedience and rebellion, by introducing an element of freedom from the dictates of God.

At Eden, everything created was under the dictates of man including the serpent, but man was under the dictates of God. The devil, through the serpent, purposed to flip the order. He knew there was no place for him in the arrangement at Eden, so the only way to smuggle himself into the equation was to get man to rebel against God, and he cashed in to the freedom of choice that man had, and wrecked the relationship man enjoyed with God which he did not have.

Any suggestion of freedom that is achieved by disobedience is not a good suggestion, and any freedom so achieved is not going to last long. If at all it is freedom, the best it can be is pseudo-freedom. By yielding to that devilish idea, man gave up servant-hood of God and became slave to the devil. In any case, all man achieved was switch from the rule of one kingdom to another. But man had the choice to have stayed in tune with God and enjoy the provisions in Eden. He did not know what he was getting himself into. He did not do a proper cost-benefit analysis. Oh, if Adam had known, he would not have given in to his wife's suggestion. It is very good to love your wife and to listen to her, but if you love your wife more than you love God, may I announce to you that you will "stumble" big time in your walk with Him. The same is applicable to wives. ..

Did you see that even if he was there in the garden he was not part of that devilish conversation? Was it not their freedom that they exercised? The free exercise of freedom could come latched with far-reaching disastrous consequences, because the creator designed us to see in part and to know in part. The fall of man introduced another parameter in the equation, and left God with choices...either to banish man from his agenda, or to redeem him with a price. God chose to redeem man but by sending His son, so that left man with a choice, either to receive Him and be saved or reject Him and be eternally damned.

It is no brainer that we want to be saved…everybody wants to be saved, but there is a way that leads to salvation and ways that lead to damnation. When a doctor writes a prescription for amoxicillin and the patient decides that he has amlodipine in the house so, why waste money instead of take what he has after all they are all medicine; do we need a prophet to tell us it will do him no good? It will probably drop his blood pressure so bad he dies quicker from it than he would have died from the disease that necessitated the amoxicillin prescription in the first place.

MUCH ADO ABOUT FREEDOM

The wisdom of this world is foolishness to God. In the sense the world talks about freedom, our freedom is restrictive. In the sense the scripture talks about freedom, our freedom is boundless. The former refers to physical freedom, the later to spiritual freedom. Why the difference? "If the son of God sets you free, you are free indeed" did not refer primarily to political, socioeconomic, financial or other kinds of freedom people want and pursue. It refers to freedom from eternal damnation reserved for those who refuse to "look unto Jesus" and be saved. When Moses made the serpent and hanged it on the tree, whosoever that was bitten and looked unto it was saved. It probably made no sense, and people had the freedom to refuse to "look" and of course the freedom to die, period. When Jesus came, the Jews thought he had come to set them free from the Roman tyrants. They were offended at him because their expectations were not met, and they were both disappointed and frustrated.

Jesus did not come to secure political independence-even though that is a good thing to have. Political independence belongs to this realm, but the kingdom that Jesus represents is not of this realm. While Jesus cares about our welfare here on earth as long as this firmament lasts, he cares even more about our eternal abode because our stay in this realm is temporary. His rulership and kingdom are not of this world, but in obedience to civil authorities, He gave unto Caesar that which belonged to him.

Apparently the Jews did not comprehend that Jesus represents a different kingdom, and so approached issues the way the kingdom he represents approaches them. "He that is from above is above all"...they were offended in him. His approaches could not have won the vote of the day. His teachings were mainly in parables, and not everybody understood what this "babbler" talked about. But He constantly, consistently and continuously fellowshipped with His father in heaven, and took instructions and directives. He submitted His will and said "nevertheless, your will, not mine, be done". Is that freedom?

Jesus, in his earthly ministry, was not free the way the world wants freedom. As we said earlier, He admonished us to give unto Caesar his portion, and to God His portion. "Love the brotherhood, fear God, honor the emperor". Caesar was a political leader, in Rome and his domain was over the whole world. Jesus submitted to authorities as a human and a noble citizen. He exercised his civil responsibilities and even paid his taxes as and when due. He even had to orchestrate miracles to make sure himself and his men were not delinquent. It is our civil duty to comply with rules and regulations, laws and the constitution, and to obey those in authorities, whether secular or ecclesiastical. Although Jesus was an ecclesiastical leader with appreciable political influence, he understood the principles in the kingdoms and the boundaries.

When he was arrested, his disciples were shocked that he did not lift his voice or finger to defend himself. He could have called fire from heaven or smitten the people with blindness, but he freely chose to die, even on the cross. He laid down his life for his beloved. He understood the ignorance of those with him, who probably wondered why he did not allow his disciples to defend him by freely adopting worldly defense strategies. Even when Peter cut off the ear of one of them that came, he picked it up and fixed it back because he understood his mission, and knew that he was going to die even for Malchus.

The kingdom to which you belong determines the methodology you adopt in your approach to life, issues and challenges. When you belong to the earthly realm, you think worldly, when you belong to the heavenly realm, you think godly…those are two parallel schools even in the definition of freedom. For example, the earthly school teaches you tit for tat, but the heavenly school teaches you to turn the other cheek when you are slapped on one. That does not make sense to those of us operating from this realm. How about "you are in the world but you are not of the world"? The wisdom of God is foolishness to men, so is the preaching of the cross to those who are perishing, but for those who are being saved, it is the power of God and the wisdom of God. The wisdom of God is available to those who will freely choose to ask of Him, now.

Even when God wants to grant a people political freedom, he does it in a different and sometimes unpredictable manner. He often uses the foolish things of the world to confound the wisdom of the wise, the mighty and the respected among men. Let us consider the exodus of the Israelites again. Moses did not know all the details of what God planned to do in Egypt, all he knew was that God was going to deliver Israel like He said He would.

If you look at the plagues, even Moses could not have thought about the elements that God used to fight Egypt. That is why it is better for us to let God deal with our enemies himself…believe me He knows how to handle them better than we can ever imagine. The anointing that raises the dead can also kill. Freedom can make you, it can also break you beyond remedy. However, the only sure freedom is the freedom that God himself orchestrates, in his own time, in his own way. To get the result we desire, we need to partner with God in our quest for freedom.

CHAPTER 3

THE MISCONCEPTIONS

Freedom is not free. By this, I am being a little bit ambiguous. (A) Freedom is not free in the sense that it costs something (B) Freedom is not free living – doing what you want, when you want it, where you want it and with whom you want it. As a matter of fact, there is no better definition for bondage than the above definition. (C) Freedom is not free meals – he that will not work let him not eat.

FREEDOM IS NOT FREE - we already talked about Jesus securing freedom from eternal damnation for us, but he paid with his blood. Even in the secular and political realm, let me use a few people this generation celebrates to illustrate. Nelson Mandela stood against apartheid and everything it represents. He invested most of his otherwise productive youthful years incarcerated. He was bounded by the four walls of the prison yard but the reach of his imagination for apartheid-free South Africa was boundless. His children grew up without their father being involved in their daily lives, chores and affairs – no school run, my son has a game this weekend, it is our daughter's birthday, or our wedding anniversary etc. You think that was not enough emotional torture?

Martin Luther King Jnr was untimely translated to eternity at the prime of his youthful life because he championed what we call freedom, again in the sociopolitical terrain. He had a dream, and followed his dream, but what did he gain in return? His wife became a young widow and his children fatherless. Again, they did not enjoy hanging out with daddy on a cool weekend out on the beaches of Florida, South or North Carolina. Today, many people enjoy a semblance of freedom because people like that died probably without enjoying it themselves. He lost his freedom in an attempt to gain freedom for his people. Even the freedom to live life was denied him at a tender age.

The people that started the move for political independence for the United States, Nigeria and South Africa for example did not all live to witness it. For example, most of Mandela's men and comrades died before apartheid was abolished. Let nobody ask me what happened to those who conceived, initiated and institutionalized apartheid. We pray that God forgives them because they did not know what they were doing. The fact that the world celebrates the life of Mandela and was reunited by his death is enough testament to the fact that the idea of apartheid is undoubtedly hellish.

Some of the men that conceived the idea of independence in the United States did not reap the dividends, but they invested for posterity. Anytime a man champions a move that promises somebody some kind of freedom or another, he steps on big toes. Those are not toes you step on and go scot free. When you tamper with status quo, you tamper with the people that benefit from and insist on status quo. If you say you want independence for example, what you say is that you want to rule yourself. It means you look somebody eyeball to eyeball and say "I don't want to report to you or be accountable to you anymore". You technically say "I don't want to pay taxes to you anymore, get the "hell" out of my territory and leave my resources alone". That is not a friendly statement no matter how friendly you try to present it. You risk having an army unleashed on that territory to which you are requesting sovereignty.

In his book "There Was a Country", Chinua Achebe talks about Biafra, the part of the world where I was born, and incidentally grew up. A people were being massacred in this amalgam, the map of which was decided by the colonial masters, without any intention to consider how it affected the people. As far back as 1914, the decision of London was executed by Lord Frederick Lugard, ethnic issues and differences notwithstanding – and Nigeria became one country. One would risk having his head cut off for daring to challenge such a selfish political maneuver. By 1967, the full result of the amalgamation reared its ugly head leading to what is considered the worst genocide of the century. Biafra came into light as a child of necessity, but not without the price for demanding freedom without weapons of warfare. Chukwuemeka Odumegwu Ojukwu led the unsuccessful attempt at freedom for his people. The rest, they say, is history.

FREEDOM IS NOT FREE LIVING – in the sense of doing what you want. If everybody does what they want, this will be a lawless society. Believe me, you and I do not want to live in a lawless society. Think about living in the hood, and what hoodlums can do even with all kinds of policing going on in inner cities. In the three countries I have lived as an adult, I have witnessed what the hood looks like. Whatever you call it or however you describe it, I can tell you it's replica in one of these countries. I will not tell you what I read in books, I will tell you what I witnessed and experienced in person and you are welcome to go and verify it.

In one occasion, I moved from one city to the other and was renting a brand new car for the first month before my car arrived. I didn't know that some hoodlums in the neighborhood were not happy to see a brand new car. They probably watched me go out and come back, and didn't know what to say or how to approach me. Apparently, they wondered what I was doing in their hood.

One early morning, as I came out to leave for work, I saw something hanging on the handle of the driver's door of my car. In Africa, I would have concluded that it was juju. On close examination, we discovered it was a used condom, hanging on my car handle. Are you kidding me, I wondered at my friend who was as shocked as I was?

Anyways, my days in that neighborhood were quickly numbered. Whosoever kept the used condom on my car handle definitely overstepped the bounds of his freedom, but was very lucky because I did not catch him. The law would have taught him lessons of life. Imagine if there is no law or law enforcement. In countries where there are very weak law enforcement, hoodlums do all kinds of unimaginable things with impunity. Have you not heard about the two hundred plus girls that were allegedly abducted by the terrorist group in northern Nigeria, leading to the global agitation for "#BringBackOurGirls"? Without adequate control, deadly weapons have been smuggled into the wrong hands, and the resultant effect is terrorism with impunity.

Beware what you want when you clamor for freedom. If you get what you are asking for, you may be shocked at the monster you get.

FREEDOM IS NOT DOING WHAT YOU WANT WHEN YOU WANT IT. Everybody wants to decide for himself when to do what he wants to do, but that will never happen. He that pays the piper dictates the tune. You don't call the shots unless you are the boss, and you don't ignore orders and expect not to be punished for it. That is the way things work in this realm. However, that you are the boss does not also give you the absolute freedom to be bossy.

I do not want to wake up early in the morning, but I have to jump up from my bed once my alarm goes off. I can complain all I want. It does not matter if I am dreaming and enjoying myself in heaven. That dream must give way for reality even on a cold winter morning when I have to go to work, regardless of whether the whole city is covered with ice or snow.

Once my schedule is made, that is it. My alarm is set to abide by my schedule which has been made, most times by somebody else, who has what I need. That person calls the shots – it could be my boss, my client or their representative. In making my schedule, they do not take into consideration my wife's schedule to make sure they are complementary. In fact, they don't care if I am a morning person or afternoon person. What my preferences are, if ever considered, are secondary to the business needs. Now I know how much freedom we all have.

FREEDOM IS NOT DOING WHAT YOU WANT TO DO, WHEN YOU WANT TO DO IT AND HOW YOU WANT TO DO IT. Most organizations have standard operating procedures (SOP) and daily operation manuals. When you get hired, you get copies of these documents. If you don't want to be fired, you will do well to take some time to study those documents and ask questions about things you don't quite understand. Most times, they have an orientation officer who would talk you through some of the key elements of those documents and give you opportunities to make sure you understand what you are getting yourself into. Those documents become your companion in the months and years to follow, and your adherence to the provisions in those documents determine your future in the organization.

Even in the same industry, regulated by the same agencies, and doing similar businesses, the SOP could still differ remarkably. Experience in one is useful in the other but does not necessarily preclude training for any new hire. When I was hired in one of the places I have had the privilege to work, my employer paid me for a whole week to get training, both in person and by way of the computer simulations. Some companies send people abroad, just to get the required training to do things the way they want it done. Sometime, the more training you receive, the more regimented you become.

One of the reasons people do not enlist in the armed forces is that they are regimented in operation. Let me tell you that the marketplace is even getting more highly regimented now. There are certain ways to do or not to do certain things, and you better know it. Knowing where the landmines are is all plus, no minus. For example, as a pharmacist, filling prescription is much more than sticking a label on a product and handing it over to a patient, like most patients think. If I made the laws, there are certain things I would do differently, but until then, I'd better obey the laws in place. Otherwise, my days as a pharmacist will be numbered. The same is applicable to every profession that is regulated. Even in the industry, the day you ignore your company's policies on issues, you will likely be written up, and your punishment could be anything from verbal warning (which is documented anyway) up to termination. The worst way to leave a job is to be fired. The psychological, emotional and economic impacts are enormous.

So while you exercise your freedom, maybe as a manager, you abide by the organization's rules and policies. If you do it how you want, you will get what you don't want in return. Sometime you don't agree with the law or policy, but you still have to obey it else you lose your job or your license or both. You probably have figured out it is better to lose a job than to lose a license. So you'd better let the angry customer call your boss and level all sorts of misconstrued allegations against you, than for anything to bring you before your professional board on allegations of gross misconduct. This is applicable, whether you sell meat at the abattoir, a medical doctor at state house clinic or a pilot on Ogbunka Airlines. It does not matter if all you do is barb hairs and clip nails. You don't do things just how you want to do them, even if you own the business.

If you are a public servant like I am, the public is your boss. If you have everybody else but you as the boss, you know you are in for a stressful career. They will stress you out, curse you out, and chew you out, day in day out. The public has a questionable expectation of what she wants from you and your business, because she pays your bills.

Some mean ones will tell you this is what they want, or they take their business elsewhere. You will have to make a decision sometime to serve them the way they want to be served, based on what makes sense to them, and the way the law and/or your company policy expects you to serve them. Sometime, the parties involved are at variance with each other on how a particular matter should be approached, so you have to decide whose punishment you can handle. This is where you cash in to experience, a good knowledge of the issues involved in that setting and the grace of God. Does that sound like you have a lot of freedom?

FREEDOM IS NOT DOING WHAT YOU WANT TO DO, WHEN YOU WANT TO DO IT, HOW YOU WANT TO DO IT AND WITH WHOM YOU WANT TO DO IT. This is bondage defined by reverse logic. A man who defines freedom in those words will not live long. If perhaps he lives long enough to have children, he will not leave any meaningful legacies behind him. Only time separates him from untimely exodus from this terrain.

The elders of my village say that a child who will live long is known from infancy. In another adage, it is said that a chick that will become rooster is identified even from the egg. It is in the house of a weakling that they stand to point at the desolated house of a strong man. "Oh, there used to live a man who was the most dreaded in the land".

Nobody does what he wants with whomsoever he wants and still expects not to pay full price for it. A certain man who was otherwise adjudged to be very responsible was sentenced to many years in prison for having affairs with minors. Had he done that with adults, nobody would have bothered; neither would it have made the news headline. All he may have to deal with would be his wife who would have to decide what is more beneficial for her and her family.

On a related issue, a man slept with his step-daughter (his wife's daughter) and impregnated her. In a culture where a child born out of wedlock is considered a bastard, I do not know what this particular child born out of "incest" would be called. In any case, the elders of the land banished the man for seven years. If he had done that with some unrelated women in the community, the story would not have survived beyond the birth and first few years of the baby. Even though the child is still considered a bastard in that culture, the stigma is nothing more than jesting and cajoling at the beer-parlor.

If the woman is unmarried, he could even go ahead and pay her bride price and take her as his second, third or fourth wife as the case may be. Who cares? The culture tolerates it and that shuts the door against any gossips or malicious comments, and in most cases the child is not a bastard. So even within that free setting, there are rules that must be obeyed for peaceful cohabitation. The boundaries are clearly defined.

There are people you don't mess with even if you are drunk. If you mess with them in your drunken state, chances are that you will be scared to ever get alcohol close to your lips again, because the lessons will live with you for the rest of what is left of your life. Your freedom has limits…it is tethered. You must know where the boundaries are even if you are sleeping, drunk or mad. Lot was drunk and had incest with his daughters which resulted in the Ammonites and the Moabites. Abraham slept with his housemaid even though it was his wife's idea, which resulted in Ishmael and his descendants…a great people but of a different ideology. It doesn't matter whose idea it is. Adam ate the fruit of the forbidden tree but it was his wife that gave him, yet he was unexcused. "Therefore thou art inexcusable oh man".

David snatched Uriah's wife and killed the man, but paid dearly for it and still paying. His descendants after him are reaping and paying for it. One would have thought that kings are above the law, like some of the kings of today that make and change laws for the common people at will. Were there not many beautiful women in the land under King David? Was he restricted in how many he could marry? Kings enjoy a lot of privileges, but those do not include taking somebody else's wife. That was an abuse of position, and all abuses are subject to punishment, now or later. Those in authority should learn from that experience. You cannot use your position to abuse, oppress, suppress, subjugate or annihilate a person or group of persons. You cannot do whatever you want with whom you want because you have the power, the position and the will to do it.

Sampson hanged out with Delilah and died like a chicken even though he was born a Nazarite to be a deliverer for his people. The Philistines messed up his destiny because he used his freedom as an occasion for lasciviousness. Did he not have freedom to date whosoever he chose? Well, I guess not. He refused to hearken to the voice of reason and the counsel of his parents like most young people do. They appeal to their peers as they accuse their parents of being rude, domineering, controlling abusive etc. In a perverse generation, even a ten year old boy claims he knows his rights, and is ready to fight for "freedom". I wonder where we are heading with this mentality.

FREEDOM IS NOT DISRESPECTFUL. We live in a generation that has little or no respect, both for the individuals and the institutions. Growing up in the 80s, we were taught to greet our seniors as soon as we meet them. Today, it is different. Young people meet their parents, or uncles, instead of saying "Good afternoon dad or mum or uncle", they walk bye without even a word to acknowledge their senior. If you remind them to greet, they say "Hi Uncle" with a nonchalant attitude. One actually told me that they were told to not greet anybody who has not greeted them. So when I meet a young boy many years my junior, I say 'good morning sir' and he says 'good morning'. Really? Is that how quickly the greeting has flipped over the years?

Different cultures have different ways of showing respect. We were taught that you don't extend your hand to shake a lady unless she extends her hands first to shake with you. When shaking hands with an elderly person, you use both hands even though you use one hand for your mates, and you bow down in respect for the age of the elderly. In that culture, age is very much valued and respected. It is believed that if you want to grow grey hairs, you must respect those who already have grey hairs. Makes sense, right? If God has respected a person by the gift of long life, you think that is not a virtue worthy of celebration, and to be held in honor?

You don't call your parents or your seniors by their first names. Even in the marketplace, sometime I find it difficult to call my staff who are as old as my mother by their first names. In my culture, we call them some kind of names depicting respect for their age and position in life and the society. Example, Deede (big brother), Daada (big sister), or you call them by their titles if they have and cherish any example. Nze, Ogbuehi, Nnabuenyi, Chinyelugo etc.

Bottom line is that what you call a person and how you call it can depict affection, respect and decorum. That also means that you don't talk while your senior is talking, and you don't talk back to them. Talking back is rude, and the cultures did not encourage rudeness under any guise. The incessant cases of people calling their fathers by first name make me sick to my stomach. In England, I met a young man who owned a business and his father worked for him. Until I was told, I could not have believed that was his father. He commanded and ordered him around like his mate. Your father is not your mate, and the fact he works for you does not give you the freedom to command him around. It doesn't matter that he lives in your house and you pay all the bills.

Children who misbehaved are punished in some commensurate ways. Although people have abused children, that does not rule out the place for godly correction. "The head of a child is bound with foolishness; the rod of correction drives it away". It is by way of correction that a child is brought up in wisdom. If freedom means that a child cannot be disciplined, how then is he going to grow up in wisdom? Are we surprised that the society in our generation is out of order? The society is made up of people, and if the people are out of order themselves, then what?

Why do we need so much policing to do the right things and to do things right? Why do we need more cameras than there are people to enforce basic etiquette? Why do we have too many laws and complicated legal systems to interpret them? Is that alone not at variance with the freedom we so much talk about?

FREEDOM IS NOT LAZINESS. Some people want to hide under freedom to be lazy. If you ask them to do a thing, they claim you are yelling, so they don't want to do it because 'he yelled at me'. Then you let them use their initiative, they say you don't have good management and leadership skills. You give them detailed instruction and monitor each step, they say he micromanages me and that makes me feel incompetent. You write them up for failing to carry out instructions; they say you are so mean and unfriendly. You fire them, they say you are insensitive and discriminatory. Whatever you do or do not do, it is your fault, and somebody is going to use that as an excuse.

"This is a free world, and nobody should take away my freedom". Have you heard that before? I agree with that position, so long as you are free to live and work for and by yourself. What actually happens is that people want you to pay the bills, but let them call the shots under the guise of this monster called freedom. Unfortunately, that is not the way things work. Is that not the reason many people cannot keep a job for two consecutive months, or be married for the same length of time?

Nothing happens unless you make it happen. A lazy man can see danger everywhere diligent people see opportunities. "I went by the farm of a lazy man, they are outgrown by weeds". The lazy observe the winds, and the weather. They watch the news channels for excuses not to go to work. I have been young, now I am old, I have never seen a lazy man that does not live in penury, whether in Africa or in America. In fact, it is said that the god of a lazy man does not exist.

I don't care how much freedom you think you (should) have, it does not immune you from the adverse effects of laziness. During planting season, some people plant a thousand yams and they tell you they planted five thousand. That is good and fine, so long as we both agree that during harvest, by the time they have finished harvesting the thousand they planted, they will begin to harvest lies to make up the difference. That is self deceit from the idle mind of a lazy bone. Get up from your bed, and go to school. Get going on that homework. Stop being a "dry" person. Otherwise, you will know no freedom from economic hardship.

CHAPTER 4

HUMANITY AND SLAVERY

As we said earlier, freedom means different things to different folks. A slave sees freedom as being able to live his life, and have the opportunities to take up his own destiny in his hands. In other words, freedom to him is deliverance from the dictates of another, probably more foolish fellow who has taken him captive and put some yoke on his ankles by reason of some discriminatory institutionalized policies, laws or treaties. For example, In Genesis we see the Israelites go down to Egypt during the seven years of famine when Joseph was Prime Minister. It was a move for survival, and fulfillment of the dreams Joseph had as a small boy in the house of Jacob. By his son's invitation, Jacob was happy to go and see Joseph, so all his descendants moved to Goshen and had a state welcome. It was a pleasant sojourn until a Pharaoh that "knew not Joseph" arose in the land.

You mean a Pharaoh did not know about Joseph or he did not know Joseph? Although Joseph was dead, his exploits lived on. In fact, all that Joseph did in Egypt have not been forgotten till this day. In Exodus 1:6-7, 18 the

Bible reads "“[6]Now Joseph and all his brothers and all that generation died,…[7]but the Israelites were exceedingly fruitful; they multiplied greatly, increased in numbers and became so numerous that the land was filled with them….[18]then a new king, to whom Joseph meant nothing, came to power in Egypt…"(NIV). He dealt treacherously with them, made them to suffer by subjecting them to harsh labor. He feared that Israel will take over Egypt if they continue to increase and prosper unchecked. He knew very well, all the exploits of Joseph but had no respect for what Joseph represented, because he was not an Egyptian, let alone from the royal family. If he knew not Joseph, how did he know that the Israelites were foreigners in Egypt? Where did he grow up? How did he even become king? Was he just being intoxicated and corrupted absolutely by absolute powers?

Do we not have people today who still think about foreigners or people of other colors as good for slavery only? Have you not worked with colleagues, managers and even subordinates who think your accent is not good enough for you to be in charge? Have you not seen people who think they should use you, take advantage of you and you must not talk after all you should be happy that you are in this country? If you haven't seen them, so be it.

Pharaoh was jealous of the prosperity of the people of God, and took drastic steps to institute laws at limiting them. Everywhere and every place, one form of the law or the other is made to restrict prosperity among immigrants. Yet, everywhere even in scriptures, immigrants tend to prosper even more than most of the so called indigenes, most of who are indigents or dependent on social services anyway.

The healthy worker effect and the immigration rules may have a part to play in that no country wants to grant visa to anybody who will be dependent on public funds. It makes absolute sense, and nothing to grudge about. It used to be what they called transparent ceiling, but now it is very opaque because immigrants are free, but they know the boundaries of that freedom. In Egypt at the time, even the small freedom they had was taken away and the people suffered under slave masters.

For four hundred and thirty years, Israelites wished, desired and prayed for freedom. Those were very long years, it probably felt like forever. You know how long the night is when you are in pain and cannot sleep? Have you been very thirsty and there is no water anywhere to drink? A minute feels like an hour, and an hour feels like a year. That was how those four hundred and thirty years dragged by until Moses showed up.

Meanwhile, the Israelites did not forget that they came. From scriptures, we understand that Jacob lived about seventeen years in Egypt before he died, but he did not forget to request his children to bury him in his country. Even Joseph, though buried temporarily in Egypt, was to be exhumed at exodus. That is culturally, sociologically and ecclesiastically significant. I see a lot of resemblance between that culture and the culture of the Igbo people of Nigeria. The head of the Igbo man does not rest until he is laid to rest in his father's compound. In the west, people think about the cost of transporting the corpse and all that. In Igbo land, the people don't care how much it costs. I am not saying that it is a good or bad thing; I am only saying that it is one of the cultures that support the claim that Igbos are Jews in diaspora.

Let us not forget that it was the prosperity of the Israelites, both in number and wealth that provoked the Pharaoh to take steps aimed at stopping them. Now, anytime you advance in a foreign country, expect opposition. Even in different parts of the same country, ugly situations like this arise.

In western Nigeria for example, how many times have the Alaye people in Lagos invaded people's goods in the name of area boys? In Northern Nigeria, how many times have the Boko Haram and similar radicals wasted lives and properties of people who came from other parts of the country? In Minna, Niger State of Nigeria a few years after my national service, other religious radicals and hoodlums invaded the Christian Corpers' Fellowship secretariat and set it ablaze killing several young graduates including an only son of his parents who came back from London to serve his fatherland. Was there no police or Army in the city to rescue these peaceful, armless and harmless citizens? In Port-Harcourt, following the Nigerian civil war that ended in 1970, all the Igbo's (Biafrans) were forced to forsake all their houses and assets to the infamous "abandoned property" policy of the state. Was that not why Dr Sam Mbakwe was dubbed "the weeping governor" as he sobbed over the fate and predicament of the Igbo-man in the post-war reintegration negotiations?

Going to Egypt was good news and a great idea. The forefathers were excited about the opportunity as it promised life and wealth, comfort and the provisions of life. It was, for Jacob, an opportunity he never thought about having, which was to be reunited with his son thought to have been dead for several years. Jacob could hardly believe that Joseph was alive, let alone being in charge of the food bank. Going down to Egypt actually provided what it promised until the prosperity of the people of God provoked ungodly policy against them.

Jacob went down to Egypt hastily. Every parent wants to hear good news from their children. When they turn the pages of the paper, they want to read about their children's exploits. It gladdens their hearts, and adds years to their days. You may not send them money, but they are happy with you. They tell their friends, and give testimonies in their gatherings. Whether you like it or not, anytime you begin to prosper and multiply, people you thought were friends and neighbors would turn into monsters in your neighborhood.

In Egypt, Joseph was free and influential. He had risen above the people he previously served. His requests were commandments that must be obeyed. Although he was second in command, there was none like him, not even Pharaoh. Why? He had the Spirit of God. It is the Spirit of God that opened the door and granted him freedom. Liberty is not gotten by killing all the other people, it is gotten by connecting with God. Today we struggle to be in the good books of the government in power, so as to get contracts and promotions. There is nothing wrong with getting promotions, but not by all means unfair. For Joseph, he remained tuned in to God even in prison. He went to sleep one day a prisoner, and woke up the next day a Prime Minister.

It doesn't take several events to become relevant to your generation. If you stay in your place of assignment, your day will come and you will shine forth. However, you must understand purpose. You must learn to let go and let God have His way. You must learn to say sincerely "may the will of God be done".

When Joseph left the prison, he forgave the people and the system that put him behind for an offence he never committed. Bitterness is a barrier to fruitfulness. If Joseph did not forgive, he probably wouldn't have become the Prime Minister. Even if he became, he would still have been in prison even as a prime minister...this time it would be self imposed prison. Un-forgiveness from the events of yesterday could deter you from the purposes of God for your life today. The weight of un-forgiveness is so heavy it doesn't let your spirit come up to the frequency that communicates with God. If you wonder why you are not getting signal from heaven, do an un-forgiveness check in your inner man. Do you know that refusing to forgive yourself could be a barrier for you too? If you have messed up, get up, pick up the pieces of yourself, forgive yourself and move on. You are not yet perfected, and you are a work in progress. God has not finished with you yet. On this side of eternity, you will never be perfect.

Yesterday is gone, bury it. You suffered injustice, hatred, etc but you are alive today. Thank God for the privilege of being able to survive, and move on. If you continue to hold unto yesterday, your tomorrow will never come, and you cannot see the provisions for today. Today has come with a lot of opportunities and privileges, only for those who have left yesterday to embrace today. There is more bondage in un-forgiveness than there is when confined within the four walls of a prison. Stop looking for freedom outside, generate it from inside.

Think about Joseph in the house of Potiphar and his wife. What happened to them when Joseph became Prime Minister? The tide had turned, and the last had become the first. For as long as Joseph reigned in Egypt, Potiphar's wife knew she had made a big error. It was, and still is common to tell lies against immigrants, and house boys and get them into trouble. Even in your neighborhood, somebody who thinks he is a citizen and does not like you could run you out of the estate if you are not financially buoyant and adequately connected in the community. If they don't say you packed your cars illegally, they would say your dog barks all night long. If your lawn is not properly mowed, maybe it is your flowers that were not properly hedged. It's got to be one thing or another and the city council would send you one letter after the other. Even if you retain the services of an attorney, how far can you go and how safe are your children in that neighborhood especially when you are not home?

Every immigrant has a different kind of story to tell. People who don't like you fabricate lies and stories to put you in trouble. Those who like you but cannot have you do the same. They come up with lies, gossips and unfounded tales to make sure nobody else talks to you. If you ever get a traffic ticket or appear in court for any form of judgment, you are assumed guilty until proved otherwise. You may not even be able to defend yourself because probably half of the jury cannot understand your accent.

Therefore every allegation against you is true even before it is verified, and nobody would give you the benefit of doubts. No, don't even expect it because it may not come. Joseph did not get the benefit of doubts. He was sent straight to prison for allegedly making advances to the wife of his master. Have you not heard about stories like this around you? Anyway, guess what? Potiphar's wife did not get what she wanted either. If she had the opportunity as in the case of John the Baptist, she would have probably asked for Joseph's head in the platter. But God kept Joseph, even in the prison. He found favor before the prison mates and the warders, because of who he was. He found the favor he needed. He didn't need favor from Potiphar and his wife because they could not have given what they didn't have – the Prime Minister's job.

Sometime you go down before you go up. Joseph did not know that the prison was the gateway to his rising. That very day he was put in prison was the day his journey of freedom from slavery started. That was the last day Mrs. Potiphar would send him on errands and give him commandments. So there could be freedom, even in the prison.

For freedom is the absence, not of fettered hands, but of fettered minds. That is one way to argue that freedom is not just physical, it could be more psychological, mental, and emotional than it is about limitations within four walls. If Potiphar's wife knew she was sending Joseph on the journey of his destiny, she would not have accused him falsely. Again, they planned it for evil, like his brethren, but God planned it for good. Hold on to your dreams, and let not circumstances deter you from reaching your goals.

Your attitude to foreigners can determine what happens to your country and to your regime. Be careful with foreign policies. If you toy with it, it will toy with your legacy. When you mess with strangers on your gate, you mess with the opportunities they bring. Their wealth of experience, their diversity and their input to your company's GDP could be very tangible.

When Joseph became PM, where were Potiphar and his wife? Did you hear any mention of them anymore, or their children? They all became subjects to Joseph. He could have turned around and made them gate keepers, hewers of wood and fetchers of water…but he (supposedly) forgave them. He let their consciences deal with them. He was going up, they were going down.

What about the cup bearer of the king that forgot Joseph after his dream was interpreted and he was restored? He was still probably bearing cup, both for the king and for Joseph, but he must also be ashamed of himself too for quickly forgetting his past like most of us do. Selfish people are very forgetful, especially when it concerns the welfare of somebody else. Joseph amply illustrates that life is very unpredictable and freedom could be a big gift that comes in small packages.

ISRAEL RESETTLES IN EGYPT

Back to his family in Egypt, Joseph requested and had them settled in Goshen, a small town within the neighborhood. Goshen eventually became a small London. By living in Goshen outside the rest of Egypt so to speak, Israel still had the freedom to worship their God and observe their cultures without interfering with the life of the Egyptians. In other words, they were in Egypt but not of Egypt. They were as close as they needed to be to the source of food, but as far as they needed to be from the culture and the gods of the Egyptians. They did not lose their identity.

Identity is very important. Who you are is more important than where you are because you can lighten up the place you are if you have light in you. "For the light shines in darkness, and darkness does not comprehend it". The right place means nothing without the right person(s). The differences between two places are the people that live in them.

As years went by, Israel increased greatly and multiplied geometrically. They became so prosperous that the Egyptians envied them. They must have been tops in their classes and occupied key positions in the affairs of the land, especially given that Joseph was not just an MP but the PM.

When Joseph interpreted the dreams of Pharaoh, they did not realize he had a different accent. If they heard his accent, nobody cared. They knew he was a foreigner and a slave boy, yet those were past tenses. I challenge all immigrants to solve problems and see if they will not be recognized and celebrated. If you do not have answers to the questions of the people, why would they celebrate you? Some of the top doctors in the US have accent, yet people go to them. Why? One of my mentors is a top cardiologist in this great country, but the high and mighty come to him despite his color, his accent and all that. Even in the city, he is a voice with which to reckon and he has audience with the high and mighty. Freedom comes by advancing in knowledge, and applying your knowledge to solve problems for humanity.

CHAPTER 5

DELIVERANCE ORCHESTRATED

Moses left his wife and sons behind and came up to Egypt to demand the release of his people. It was like going up to the king of England or signing letters addressed to the King of England demanding independence for the United States or any of the British colonies. You must be really going against the tides anytime you embark on such missions. Have you been a tenant before and at the end of your lease requested your deposit from the landlord? Did you receive the full amount?

Only once in my leasing history and my sojourn have I received my deposit in full, but not without a clear communication of my readiness to challenge any attempts to withhold my money. Landlords always come up with reasons…the floor was not clean enough, there was dust on the window, you did not refill the gas (that was never used), even though I have been made to drive up to pay $1 to connect to the Wi-Fi on the facility on a day my internet was not good.

Think about it. It was in England I asked myself "If it can be this difficult to collect deposits, how easy do you think it is to ask for freedom or deliverance from slavery or apartheid"? Can the captive of the mighty be delivered? At that stage in your life, freedom could mean having your own house and paying rents to nobody, although you may still have to deal with mortgage. For some people, the more they try, the farther away the dream gets. It feels like forever.

These idle men are asking for freedom, Pharaoh must have wondered. Over the decades, slavery had been institutionalized in Egypt that every Israelite born within that period knew where he belonged, and the limit of his aspirations. Thinking about freedom is like asking for the impossible. Mandela said "it always feels impossible until it is done". Some of them did not believe Moses' story. They wanted freedom, but they did not believe it when it was coming their way because of how and by whom it came.

Moses had to prove to them that surely, Yahweh was involved. Sometime we pray, and wish, and desire a thing but secretly doubt the possibility. At other times, we pray, echo amen but do not believe it will happen. We just can't imagine how it will be possible, and so we limit God. Did Sara want a son? Did she believe the angel that told her Isaac would be born? It did not make sense to a woman who had lived pass her menopause...but with God nothing shall be impossible.

When Pharaoh heard Moses, he was vexed. "Oga, iwe ewela gi (Master, don't get angry). God has sent us to tell you "Let my people go". Oh, now I know that you have been idle and lazy indeed. Who would make those bricks? Who would do all the menial jobs…the kind that my folks are doing in different parts of the world in search of dollars and pound sterling.

Now we are going to remove the subsidy. Bondage comes in different shapes and forms. If not that God was fully involved, it was actually a near impossible situation. Moses and Aaron would have dared it to their own peril. If the Egyptians did not kill them for daring to challenge status quo, the Israelites would have killed them for increasing their burdens by their over-zealous demands. Even with all the mighty works and miracles God did in Egypt which they all witnessed, did they not murmur against Moses and Aaron in the wilderness? Was it not in His anger that God made them wanderers until they all perished that murmured?

Pharaoh was in charge, called the shots and issued decrees until Moses and Aaron showed up with "Thus saith the Lord". They must be out of their minds, Pharaoh must have wondered. Until the plagues began to unfold one after the other, and continued until Egypt could bear it no more. Take a look at the plagues again in the book of exodus. That alone will convince you that the earth is the Lord's and the fullness thereof, the world and the people therein, including Pharaoh and all Egyptians. Again, the elements belong to God, even locusts, frogs, diseases, the water bodies, the wind, the moon etc. Who could have explained where all those frogs came from? And the locusts? The creativity of the plagues is beyond human imagination. At the end of it all, did freedom come to Israelites? Yes, but by the finger of God.

CHAPTER 6

IN SEARCH OF FREEDOM

God had to change his name to match his character. Jacob started by swindling birth right from his brother in what was the first documented high level fraud in scriptures. We understand birth rights, the provisions and the potential abuses of it. I grew up in a culture where it is unfortunately grossly abused. People who profess to be Christians hide under the so called birth right and commit untold atrocities. Jacob had to maneuver his way. In the contemporary world, the way to explain it would probably be that the father loved the first son and would have willed his possessions to him by cultural practices, so the second son and his mother plotted an overthrow of intentions. However, it was his mother's involvement that made it a success.

For him, freedom meant gaining his father's blessings, although he was afraid of attracting curses to himself if the father discovered his treachery. His mother reassures him by "your curses be upon me". As he shows up with the voice of Jacob and the skin of Esau, he gets the blessings, right? Was that the end of his need for freedom? Mankind will never be without the need for freedom. We will have no rest until we find rest in God.

Off to his uncle Laban he ran like a smart boy, heeding his mother's counsel. Under his uncle's shelter Jacob found refuge and in love with his daughter, Jacob fell. Did he not serve seven years for Rachel only to be deceived and maneuvered to marry Leah, who he did not fancy? Did he not serve another seven years for Rachel, and was he not used and cheated by Laban to advance himself? As if those were not enough, at the end of about twenty years of servitude, did he not sneak out of town with his wives and children in search of freedom from his uncle who also was his father-in-law?

Away with Laban and all his troubles, Jacob now had to appease his brother or have his head cut off, perhaps his brother was still angry with him. Did he not take thousands of gifts and rearranged his team in ways he would prefer them to die if his brother attacked? Fortunately, he found grace before his brother but before then, had to wrestle with an angel who had to break his hip bone and change his name. God had indeed blessed him, and blessing him but he lived in exile and suffered extortion for decades; all in search of freedom.

Did I say he lived abroad? That was even before he had to live abroad again in Egypt in the days of Joseph his son as Prime Minister.

JOSEPH AND HIS BROTHERS

Jacob loved Joseph and made him a coat of many colors. It was actually a transfer of the love he had for his mother, Rachel. I grew up in a culture where polygamy is practiced, so I have witnessed, and to a great extent understand some of the nuances of a polygamous setting. The western cultures do not have provisions for polygamy in their laws. However, in my sojourn to the west, I have met people who would vote for polygamy, and would marry several wives as a way to gain freedom from the one they have now. Marrying several wives as a way of freedom from one sounds like an open invitation for more troubles.

Joseph's brothers thought that if they killed him, or sold him away, they would be free from his dreams. They did not want to bow down and worship this over-zealous dreamer son of a swindler. He probably ate a good porridge one night, or had a spell of malaria attack and began to hallucinate. Let's sell him and see what would become of his dreams. Thank God that gone are the days when people are sold into slavery, many of us would have been sold over and again from hand to hand.

Joseph did not stop dreaming. His spiritual receivers were always on to download spiritually coded information. His dreams came to pass, but not without many days in Potiphar's house and in prison. From the prison, Joseph was on his way to the Prime Minister's office, which was probably why Mandela said "In my country, people go to prison before they become Presidents". He did not enjoy the limitations associated with the four walls of a prison house, and did not forget to ask the young man to remember him when he was going to be restored as a cupbearer in Pharaoh's house. But the fellow forgot. Man always forgets, and the arm of flesh always fails those who put their trust in them.

When the appointed time came, freedom came to Joseph in the prison. It also marked the beginning of freedom for Egypt from what would have been the worst disaster of the generation. In fact, that freedom also extended to Israel from what would have been the total annihilation of the Israelites. The dream of Joseph is paying off now. If he did not dream, or did not share it, they probably wouldn't have sold him. Like he rightly told them, they planned it for evil but God planned it for good to preserve life.

The freedom for which we struggle must benefit humanity. One of my associates once told me, however jokingly, that I dream big. I smiled and asked her how much more it costs to dream big than to dream small. She said "Nothing". I asked her how much bill is sent to anybody for dreaming and she said, "Nothing". Ok, Is it good to dream at all? She said "Yes". So why waste your time and energy dreaming if you would not dream big, and why dream small if it costs the same amount of resources to dream whether big or small? She thought that was smart. If you want to eat a toad, eat the big one.

Think about it, Joseph bought over the whole land of Egypt for Pharaoh (except the priest's place) in exchange for food in the seven years of famine. Under his leadership, people willingly gave up all their lands for food...that was how bad it got. Is it not because the Pharaoh that knew not Joseph inherited the whole land of Egypt that he would dare ask "Who is the God of Israel that I should obey Him?" He was like the proverbial nza (bird) that ate a good lunch and challenged his Chi (god) to a wrestling match.

ABRAHAM GOES TO EGYPT

In search of freedom, this time again from hunger and famine, Abraham goes down to Egypt and tells them his wife is his sister so they would not kill him. For a hungry man, there is no greater freedom than finding food for himself and his family. Think about the ordeals he went through and the agony of surviving in a foreign land, like many of Africa's professionals in sundry parts of the world, with a hope of going home someday which may never materialize, in life or in death. The problem is not so much about going abroad but more about being able and knowing when to go back. Go back and do what? Better go with a lot of money, but how do you get that? The challenges in one's native country are many, but the challenges in a foreign land are enormous.

Abraham went through a lot in foreign land in search of freedom, despite the special call of God upon his life. If he embarked on that journey on his own accord because it looked good, he couldn't have achieved a lot, if anything. For immigrants in my generation or those who intend to migrate, let me tell you. Even if you heard God call you by name and tell you with a very audible voice in the presence of witnesses to leave your country to a foreign land, you will likely go down before you go up. That is the way it works. That's not what you want to hear, but anything else is a lie and a misrepresentation of the truth. It is applicable, even if you win the visa lottery.

When God begins to prosper you in your new found abode, the blessings of God attract the envy of the inhabitants of the land; even those you thought are your brethren. Some of them who came before you will see you as being so much in a hurry. Others will see you as not being qualified for the blessings that come your way, because they think they have a lot more going on than you have. They think their accent is better than yours, and their college diploma more respected than yours. Bottom line is that people will take advantage of the fact you are new in the land and probably naïve in your dealings.

If you disagree with one, you probably disagreed with all. If you challenge one, you probably challenged all. If you fight with one, they will team up and gang up against you to subdue you. If they have to tell lies or accuse you falsely to run you out of town, they will probably do it. They will surely get you, either from what you did or what you did not do. On the preponderance of evidence a matter is ruled in every court. When evidence is not in your favor, do you need any prophet to tell you jail is around the corner? To be free, and freely enjoy the blessings of God in a foreign land, you need the giver of the blessing to sustain you. The name of the Lord is a strong tower, the righteous runs into it, and is safe. That is freedom.

ISAAC IN FOREIGN LAND

After the death of Abraham, did Isaac his son not suffer the same fate? Again, the Abrahamic order of blessings was upon his life, according to the promises of God to Abraham. How many times did he dig wells in times of famine, and they contended with him and took it for themselves. This was a man whose birth was announced by angels, and a direct heir of the promises of God to Abraham. He moved from place to place digging wells for them to claim until they got tired and left him alone, hence he called it Rehoboth.

God had blessed him, he had everything but freedom. "Depart from us for you are mightier than we" they said to him. When they thought he could join their enemies to fight them, they made him enter into a covenant of peace. By all means, he knew he was a foreigner to the inhabitants of the land.

He was prosperous, and they knew that God was with him, yet he still lived at the back side of town where the Lord had made room for him. He still did not do what he wanted, when he wanted and how he wanted it...he had to abide by the precepts of God, for in it did he have anything you could call peace and freedom.

SAMSON AND THE PHILISTINES

Was Samson not born to be a deliverer for his people? Was he not anointed like none before and after him? Did he not posses all the powers like none before or after him? Israel needed him so desperately to be free from the philistines, but he needed so desperately to be free from his love for strange women. Everywhere he went, he saw nothing but beautiful women. When a man loves everything with long hairs, he needs freedom more desperately than a thirsty man needs water.

Delilah was not just a person but also a character. There are many Delilah's walking about waiting for the opportunity to put somebody to spiritual sleep, and the rest will be story. Every Sampson has a Delilah to watch out for. If she gets your attention, she will not stop until you are bound, hair shaved, eyes plucked off and strength gone. If you are in the net of a Delilah, you need freedom as desperately as you can have it. He that keeps Israel, may he never sleep or slumber. We must fulfill our destinies, and we don't need any Delilah on our way.

CHAPTER 7

FREEDOM CALLS

Nobody likes to be oppressed or suppressed. God created places before he created people and he located the people he created in their rightful places and gave them precious gifts for their subsistence. In different parts of the world we see there is abundance of something or some precious elements.

The Ogoni People of Nigeria for example have great oil deposits, yet the people are so poor yet nobody seems to care about their ordeals. Huge underground pipes run from there across the country to the north where a refinery is located, even though Kaduna is yet to discover any droplet of oil in her underground water bodies. That confirms the saying that where you catch the crab is not where you wash it and clean it up.

Maybe Ogoni land is not good to build refineries, and the one in Port Harcourt has left much to be desired or discussed. To add salt to injury, we watch documentaries showing the lack of basic amenities and the dilapidated nature of primary schools and other social amenities. There is not enough to show for the oil they supply to the rest of the world, worth billions of dollars a year – another irony of life. Today, freedom from the health hazards associated with petrochemicals such as cancer is a dream in Ogoniland. Not only that, poverty, poor health and poor healthcare have become the lot of most of them as their natural sources of livelihood – fishing and farming – are grossly affected by oil expedition and spillage.

THE NIGER DELTA SAGA

Certain countries may be poor but the individuals are not poor. When you see primary school children taking classes under the mango trees, you know that is not a good sign. In a country where local government counselors earn more than state governors, and senators in developed countries, one would think some sectors like education, health, power and agriculture would be given priority. This is not just in Ogoni land, but elsewhere in the country.

When you ask them what freedom means, you will hear them refer to the oil in their land, and being able to use it to develop their land. The political-economists call it Resource Control. All manner of militant groups have arisen over the years fighting for what they think freedom should be. Injustice everywhere threatens justice everywhere. Even if the rest of us pay them reparation for air pollution, or water pollution, will they be free?

In West Texas for example, individuals who own the lands came up with a smart idea. If you buy land now to build a house, you get the right to use the surface, but the owner retains the right to the underground minerals. Can you beat that smartness? Do you not think that is fair? Why can't we do that in other parts of the world? How do we secure peace in those oil rich and troubled areas of the world? The world has seen more trouble and violence since oil became a hot commodity, and more human blood has been shed than the oil flowing in the underground water bodies, as if human blood has become an important additive to crude oil. Something to think about.

Does it sound like what happened in South Africa? How did apartheid start? To give us idea of numbers, statistics has it that about one million Ogoni people live in an area of about four hundred square miles, an area whose greatest problem has become the free gift of nature to them. There is something wrong when a people become victims of human rights violations on their own land.

The media has a way of coloring issues and events with political colorants and flavors, but that does not mean somebody somewhere does not know the truth. Just like one would also ask, "How did the idea of colonization come to the mind of men?" What is the genesis of slavery? When I asked a British Professor to explain why it was necessary to colonize a people; with an attitude that was particularly brutish he said it is only an American that would ask that question. That still didn't answer my question, did it?

Let's recall that Africans had lived their lives and gone about their businesses prior to 1889 when the British came to colonize them, and ultimately amalgamated what is now known as Nigeria into a country in 1914. Who made the decision to amalgamate these several tribes, and nations as they were, into one? Was it vetoed or voted? The difference between vote and veto is simply in the arrangement....four letters rearranged.

By 1950s, Nigerians were already agitating for independence- freedom from the colonial masters. In 1956, the British and Royal Dutch found abundant and viable oil fields in Niger Delta and began oil exploration in 1958. By 1991, it was alleged that Ogoni-land accounted for about 40% of the total oil spills of the Royal Dutch/Shell company worldwide. Oil spills, oil flaring, waste discharges, have turned the once fertile land into a public health hazard and no longer viable for agricultural use for a people who are predominantly farmers, fishermen and traders.

Every public health professional understands the health implications of environmental degradation and pollution. In an analysis of the ground water for example, very high level of hydrocarbons were detected, by far above WHO guidelines for benzene, a carcinogen. The people agitate for freedom in ways the rest of the world condemn. Again, leaving lots of unanswered moral questions.

The person who is holding unto that which belongs to you accuses you of being rude in the way you ask for what is legitimately yours. Violence is not a way to go, but why do we make peace impossible by policies and laws, hence making violence inevitable, when it becomes the only option left to pursue?

While we condemn the people for agitations, wouldn't it be better to address their legitimate, valid and reasonable concerns timely? How many environmental Impact Assessments and Health Impact Assessments have been funded and conducted in these places? As a public health advocate and an epidemiologist, I am personally concerned about the health impacts associated with acid rain; respiratory problems to which the neighboring communities are exposed, and cancer associated with high levels of benzene, a highly unsaturated carcinogenic hydrocarbon.

Anytime government is indifferent to the ordeals of a people - the hen that lays the golden egg - that calls for some kind of agitation for freedom. The arrest, sentencing and ultimate hanging of the Ogoni-Nine was condemned by the rest of us, who could have done much more than just talking about it and watching the blood of men spill as additives to the crude oil, that has dominated the economic discussions in the past sixty years. On the balance lies the life and fate of anybody or group of people who decide what freedom is to them, and set themselves out to seek it for themselves, their children and their people. Whether they seek it violently or non-violently, there is always a huge price to pay.

APARTHEID IN SOUTH AFRICA

Based on documents available in public domain, racial segregation in South Africa began in the colonial times under Dutch rule and apartheid became official in 1948 through 1994. Citizens were classified as white, black, colored or Indian and residential areas were segregated, sometime by forced removals. Non-white political representation was abolished by 1970. The segregation was seen even in education, medical care, public services, and beaches with black people getting services inferior to whites. These were happening long after the US had abolished slavery, even though it replicated most of the things that happened in the days when slavery was stark in the US. What really amazes me is how recent these events are.

Like most ventures, petty apartheid preceded the grand apartheid. Under petty apartheid, people were forced to belong to one of man-made/man-designed and designated races so much that siblings were categorized into different racial groups based on probably how they looked, their features or the fancy of whoever categorized them. How ridiculous! There was prohibition of mixed marriages act of 1949 which ruled out marriage between persons of different races while the immorality Act of 1950 made sexual relations with a person of a different race a criminal offence. Can you imagine that?

There was a reservation of separate amenities act of 1953 that separated beaches, buses, hospitals, schools and universities by color of people's skin. Inscriptions such as "Whites only" "For Black People Only", were seen everywhere. In case you do not know, The Bantu Education Act of 1953 segregated the education system in ways that South African students were prepared to live as a laboring class. In other words, they graduated from colleges prepared with skills adequate for them to occupy positions as janitors, hewers of wood and fetchers of water in their own country. If you can understand and rationalize that Israelites were hewers of wood in Egypt, how can you explain that South Africans were hewers of wood in South Africa?

In the 1960s, 70s and 80s, the government resettlement policy was enforced and people were forced to move to the designated "group areas", forcing millions of people to relocate. Imagine the inconveniences involved and the psychological and emotional trauma.

Women were grossly affected by apartheid. They suffered both racial and gender discriminations. While the black men were discriminated against, black women were simply oppressed. They had little or no legal rights, no access to education, and absolutely no rights whatsoever to own properties. Jobs were limited and even when they worked, could not negotiate better wages and had to accept extremely low remunerations. Imagine the impact on children - widespread diseases, extreme malnutrition, poor sanitary conditions, and high morbidity and mortality rates. Even birth rates among black people were restricted. Virtually all of what you and I consider fundamental human rights, choices and decisions were regulated.

Does it give you enough impression of what we are talking about on freedom? Several books and commentaries have been written on the subject of apartheid to which the reader is referred for further details. Therefore we will not dwell long on it in this book. As far as we are concerned, apartheid was simply a leadership problem. In all fairness, it was not necessary. After it was initiated, the resources and means to stop it abounded but the political will did not abound. In fact, it was lacking.

Somebody was benefiting from it and would not let it die. People prefer to protect business interests than to respect humanity or preserve life. It is one thing to have the power and ability to do something; it is another to have the will to do it. Without the will, ability is disabled and power is incapacitated. When business interest comes in the way of rational reasoning and the fear of God, everybody loses eventually.

Today it baffles to know that there are people in South Africa and elsewhere who still do not see anything wrong with apartheid; some have even dared justify slavery and discrimination with scriptures. I have travelled a bit, and met people from different parts of the world. There are human beings in this generation who still think that other people should be hewers of wood and fetchers of water, not just in South Africa but elsewhere. Come on people, it is ridiculous and probably lunatic to uphold such an opinion in the 21st century.

There are others who think that those who instituted apartheid and sustained it with public funds should be charged with crime, and sentenced howbeit posthumously. They believe that apartheid is a crime and the perpetrators are criminals regardless of their titles, positions or creeds. Guilty of the sin are also the people who kept quiet instead of support the legitimate struggle of a people to become free in their own land. Neither the former nor the later may be necessary, but a good knowledge of history is needed to avoid its repetition.

When you ask somebody who experienced apartheid to define freedom for you, you bet how he would define it.

CHAPTER 8

UNDERSTANDING PURPOSE

Certain people are considered humble and humane until they get into positions of power and influence. A man should probably be considered proud until he has tasted and been tested by power. It could be economic power, political power or ecclesiastical power. After all, pride is a by-product, not of high handedness but of high mindedness.

In Joseph, we see a humble man. His beginning was very humble. Among the children of his father, he had no recognizable position. He had no voice as far as the culture provided. He was not born into a position that could be heir apparent under any arrangements. However, his father loved him. His brethren were jealous of him, and conspired to sell him as an alternative to killing him. By all means, they couldn't stand him any longer because his dreams threatened their cultural positions and expectations.

Theirs was a culture where everybody knew where he belongs by virtue of birth. We all know that God blesses who he wants to bless regardless. For example, Esau was older, Jacob was blessed; Ruben was older, Joseph was blessed; everybody else was older, David was chosen; Manasseh was older, Ephraim was blessed. In scriptures you hear about Ephraim and Manasseh instead of Manasseh and Ephraim…how do you explain that?

Man is naturally selfish, and no man wants to bow down and worship another, let alone your junior. Even in the work place, you don't want to report to a boy that just graduated from college yesterday. In the military, people actually resign when their juniors are promoted over and above them. It is actually a modest way of telling a senior military officer "your services are no longer needed, Sir".

Joseph did nothing but serve them, taking their food and drink to the field. He happily and dutifully ran errands for their father, as he displayed his coat. That coat must have been bought for him because he was close to his father. They probably thought their father would will his inheritance to this little boy, and they wouldn't let that happen. They became jealous.

They wanted to be a step ahead of the game and to stop him by all means. This boy cannot rule over us. They forgot that rulership is not always by voting. The anointing of God that makes for rulership is not always subject to human appointment. Men can vote yet God can veto in the contrary. It is wisdom, in leadership to know when to vote and when to veto. In the house of Potiphar, he served dutifully, humbly and diligently. In prison, he served again.

He lived a life of service. The way up is down, the way to leadership is service. Great servants make great leaders.

Joseph did not wait for things to line up for him before he starts serving or living his life. He did not wait to be ordained or confirmed or appointed before he would live an exemplary life. He did not seek his elevation, neither was he ambitious. Ambition is good, but insufficient to get you to your place in destiny. Humility and service will take you far beyond where ambition and qualification will.

As a prime minister, Joseph served, not just Pharaoh but the whole people that depended on the food bank over which he saw and directed. He had the single opportunity of his lifetime to avenge himself of all the ills in his life – being sold into slavery, being falsely accused, being put in jail, and being forgotten in prison by the people he helped. This is very remarkable in a generation, as in ours, where pastors and prophets make you pay for prayers and prophecies as if they are the ones that perform the acts of God. If you come to them and God answers your prayers, they've gotten you and you must not question whatsoever they do or ask you to do, otherwise you would be labeled ungrateful, sinful and rebellious.

As soon as you have a glimpse of the answer to the prayer they prayed with you, you must come and give testimonies and thanksgiving; and you must not come empty handed. Then they grab the mega phone and get on the TV to broadcast that they have become miracle workers. Every now and then they remind you, lest you forget and rebel. Do you need a prophet to tell you there are too many people who are in dire need of freedom from these "holier than thou art" pastors and self-acclaimed men of God?

Joseph received revelation of dream and its interpretation. He was full of the Spirit- a man of God by every standard yet he did not hold anybody to ransom. He attributed his success to God and gave God the praises. Moreover, he did not forget yet he forgave freely.

When his brothers came, he knew them but they knew him not. Can you imagine all that Joseph could have done to teach them lessons? That was neither necessary nor optional. He already knew that they planned it for evil but God planned it for good, so he needed not fight or oppress them. He used his position to serve and to preserve life. Life cannot be preserved without service. More importantly, he used his position to set men free from hunger and the danger of death.

Joseph was humble but his humility was not really tested until he had tasted power and influence. If you think your friend is humble, wait until he tastes power, or becomes what he wants to be. You are campaigning for him to become the next governor of your state? That is a good idea, but wait until he gets to the government house at the capital city, then you know if he is your friend or not. By the time he changes his phone number without giving you the current one, or you wait all day at the reception because he is meeting with his girl friend, then you know the friend you have.

Those who have influence and are still available and reachable are the truly humble people. How many of those do you still have in your circle? What about you? Are you one of those that thank God for deliverance from poor friends? You probably need freedom from your mentality.

THE "COMPLEX" BONDAGE

Bondage comes in different shapes and forms. Many people are in self-imposed bondages- the superiority complex and the inferiority complex. People who think more highly of themselves and maintain an exaggerated opinion of themselves have superiority complex. They think they are better than anybody else or more beautiful, more educated, more preferred etc. The resultant effect of that is pride, arrogance, disrespect for people and disregard for rules, norms and cultures. The grand effect is idolatry - attributing the glory of God to their knowledge, connection, elegance, wisdom, or anointing.

Joseph was not like that. Do you think he was not smart? He worked very hard to maintain an excellent resume all through. Not once did we see him talking or making reference to his smartness, knowledge, dream interpretation skills, or his politically correct ways of doing things. He gave God the glory.

Superiority complex would limit anybody and everybody from advancing beyond their present status. Superiority complex has a way of complicating your life. You tend to bite more than you can chew and attract to yourself more problems than you can handle. It sets you up for failure. It scares away from you the help you need to get to your next level, as it projects you as self-sufficient. Anybody so tormented needs urgent freedom from a self-imposed prison.

The opposite is inferiority complex – people who do not think that they are good enough, smart enough, beautiful enough, educated enough, to do things or stand up against something they believe to be wrong. They compare themselves with someone else and conclude that they don't have a chance. They can give you a list of all the things they don't have, and cannot see one thing they do have.

Even when they agree to see what they have, they think nobody recons with that. They wish they were their next door neighbor who is more blessed and has a lot more going on. A person suffering from inferiority complex dies slowly but steadily of self pity. Let me announce to you that nobody is ever going to give you an award for self pity. Also, you are never going to attract enough sympathy to make anybody abandon his own life to live yours. Get excited about who you are and what you have. You need to be excited to excel. Life is too short to waste time in self pity.

Like I said earlier, one of my associates accused me of dreaming big. I asked her how much it costs to dream big, and she said "Nothing". I asked her how much more it costs to dream big than to dream small, and she said "Nothing". So why should I dream small if I don't pay any more money for dreaming big? Don't be in bondage by your own dreams. Some people are poor because they cannot dream big. They have a mediocrity mentality. Fear of failure restricts them.

Joseph dreamed big. He was neither afraid to dream nor to share his dream boldly and publicly. It does not mean he was over-ambitious like his brothers thought, neither was he afraid like most people are. There are people who are afraid to dream dreams. Others forget their dreams before they wake up from their sleep. In this kingdom, the violent takes it by force. If such happens to you, you need to get back to sleep again and demand a continuation or a replay of your dream. Get up and write it down. That becomes a prayer point. By the time you have written the vision in plain languages, you can run with it (Habakkuk 3).

Joseph rehearsed the dream to himself time and again. It filled his mind, and his heart. The mouth speaks out of the abundance of the heart. In this kingdom, you see what you say, but only when what you say lines up with what

God says concerning you. I have several personal examples. In 2005, I told some people that the day God would move me and my family to the United States, it would be all expense paid. I didn't have any idea what I talked about, and I didn't know anybody who had it so; nor did I have any idea when or how it was going to happen. In 2008, it happened just like I had "prophesied". Freedom is of God. For me, moving to the US was a form of freedom from all the negative experiences and challenges of living in the UK as a student, with a young family.

As a student leader, I had a dream about a certain member of my fellowship, concerning the things that would happen to her if she did what she was planning secretly to do. I shared it and warned her, but she did not take it seriously until several years after, she called to tell me everything I told her came to pass. I felt so bad because they were no good news and nothing to be proud about.

Before I left Nigeria for England in 2004, I had a dream about the transformations that would happen in my village in my lifetime. I shared it boldly and publicly to the annoyance of some people who think they are more spiritual than I or do not believe that God still speaks to ordinary people in dreams. While those things have not yet all happened, some of them have happened and I am still confident I will not die until I witness the rest of the things I saw and prophesied.

CHAPTER 9

THE PRODIGAL APPROACH

A certain man had two sons. From all indications, that was a very comfortable man. His two sons had everything they needed, and even things they wanted. They even had servants doing things in the house. They were free to do what they wanted under their father's house. Their contemporaries would have wished they were those boys. What freedom would you have thought they needed?

The younger of the two woke up one day to request his portion of the father's possession. The father obliged him. Everything the father had was shared and he took his own portion, and off to a distant country he went. He did not want to submit to his father, let alone his brother. Where do you hear that a man splits his wealth to his children while he is alive? Although wills are becoming very popular in contemporary societies, they don't go into effect until the man dies.

In this case, protocol was disallowed. The boy took his own portion and zoomed off to a far country. In search of freedom, he gave himself up to bondage. He lavished his possession in riotous living. That is freedom, isn't it? That is what we all consider freedom today – doing what I want, when I want it, how I want it and with whom I want it. By the time they had wasted his possessions, all his friends deserted him. Loneliness became his lot. To avoid imminent death by hunger, he gave himself over to a farmer…feeding pigs of all animals. Why pig? How did he end up with the dirtiest and nastiest of all animals? As if that was not enough insult, he would even want to eat food meant for the pigs, yet nobody gave him. He began to have a good understanding of the consequences of freedom that he sought from his father.

After the passage of time, he came to his senses, and asked himself hard questions, so he provoked hard answers. "How many of my father's hired laborers have enough and to spare and I perish here of hunger"? I will arise and go to my father, and will say unto him, "Father, I have sinned against heaven and before you…make me like one of your hired laborers'. This boy began with freedom in his father's house, took it for-granted, lost it, lived in bondage; now he wants to become a hired laborer in his father's house. When you take what you have for-granted, you get grounded.

He saw his folly and owned up to his foolishness. All the ego was gone. He began a long journey to what would become his ultimate freedom. In the journey through life, often times, you have to go down before you go up. He hit the bottom rock and would not go any further, so he looked up and got up. Anytime you look up, you are getting up. David was correct when he declared, "I will look up…" (Psalm 122). If you can look up, you can go up; if you can go up, you can be restored. "Upon Mt Zion, there is deliverance…and the children of Israel will possess their possession" (Obadiah 17).

The journey back home was long, and tiresome. He literally made a u-turn in his journey and went back up the same distance he went down. He had no strength left. He used the last energy he could muster and was practically putting one leg in front of the other. He was resolved, and he knew his father would be gracious to forgive.

He was still afar off when the father saw him and ran and hugged him. The father received his son with joy and wouldn't even let him request what he had been reciting in his mind as he journeyed home. Immediately, the father had a robe of sonship put on him. Freedom was restored to him and there was joy at home.

A son, who was dead, is now alive…what more can a father ask for? His freedom was not complete until he found it in his father's house; so our freedom is not complete until we find it in Christ. Does it now mean he can do whatever he wants? No. The rules that he rejected before his journey have not changed, but his approach to it has. Sometimes, the value of a thing is not known, until the thing is lost.

It is in unguarded moments that we ask for freedom from His dictates. Take my yoke upon you and learn of me…for my yoke is easy and my burden is lighter than the burden of sin and sinfulness. This means there is no freedom without responsibility. Responsibility is the price for greatness. Freedom does not come through riotous living and rebellion; it comes through submission to legitimate authorities.

You have to decide which yoke you want to bear, but surely there is a yoke. No one is without one, just like everybody has issues. Many teenagers cannot wait to turn 18 before they run off of their parents' house in search of freedom. Some of them get involved in a wreck and then wreck their lives and destinies because they are in a hurry to shun counsel, and to do their own bidding. It doesn't take long after you do your own bidding to outbid yourself.

Several of them drop out of school because they don't like anybody to tell them what to do. Unfortunately, you are in the wrong place. Even the president of the United States does not do only what he wants to do. Nobody becomes anything worth becoming by shunning counsel.

We probably live in a generation of prodigal sons. He invoked the freedom act like many of us do today. Does this sound like it refers to you or anybody with whom you have come in contact? The prodigal son is not just a person; he is a character that lived now then. The story is as relevant in Bible days as it is in our day. He wanted by all means, to belong.

He was not alone in that mindset because he spent his substance with his peers, who definitely held him in honor. However, when he was down, they deserted him. Both boys and girls disappeared from the scene. At some point he became ashamed. By this time, his friends who were submissive to parents, and went on to college had graduated, and probably became professionals.

Without good education, certificates, relevant qualifications, and experience what do you think you can become in this modern age? A janitor? A gardener? Was that not the job of Israelites in Egypt as slaves and bondmen? So are you free now choosing to do jobs now that bondmen did then?

The prodigal son came to himself. He discovered his mistakes. He judged himself, condemned himself, forgave himself and swallowed his ego. As soon as you discover, recover. He figured out that a recovery mission would do him good, so he went for it. Then he realized how far away from home and from dad he was. But his father did not move, he moved. His father was home and all along, looking out through the window to see, peradventure his son comes home. Each time you realize that you are far away from God and out of network, you moved. The earlier you turn around and head back home the better. If you can look up, you can go up.

We don't know how long it took him to go back home – hungry and worn out. But he kept going. He took responsibility for his actions "I am no longer worthy to be called your son. I have sinned against you". That is responsibility.

We live in an irresponsible generation – nobody wants to take responsibility especially when things go wrong. If you come to my house and slip/fall on the staircase, it is my fault because I did not turn on the lights and you neither saw nor did you care to look for the switch at the entrance door…so off to the court you go to press a charge. Really?

It snowed all day and as you passed by my property you slipped and fell, off to the court you run to file claims against me for not cleaning up the snow so you can pass on clean road. Well, I am going to court as well to press charges against you for trespassing my property, and for falling down on it. Don't you see anything wrong with this mentality? Are we not slaves to our own mentalities?

Responsibility is the mother of greatness. If you don't take responsibility for your actions, you are simply irresponsible; and nobody wants to do business with an irresponsible fellow. This is the bitter truth. As a manager, I have been written up partly because my staff closed the business fifteen minutes before closing time on a day I was off, and I didn't write them up when I came back. It was my fault. Can you believe it? I took responsibility for it.

The prodigal son comes to his father as he is. Even if he considered borrowing money or clothes, nobody would lend him. People who knew about his background would call him stupid and good for nothing. He knew all was not well and he could not pretend any longer. For how long can you pretend all is well? When you say all is well, not out of faith but out of pretence, you die in silence in the midst of help. Wouldn't that be a foolish death?

One thing about the prodigal is that he was still a son…prodigal is just an adjective – it qualified him by his action. All he needed was a change of thought and a change of action, and prodigal would be behind him, yet sonship remains his identity. So he shows up at his father's house as he is. People who saw him on the way home could have called him lunatic. Nobody would have dared shake hands with him, let alone give him a hug because he was filthy, pale looking, wearing rags.

The father hugs him as he is. It is only a good father that would have hugged his dirty self. Even a wife would probably wait until he is cleaned up and brushed up. He was quickly made over, and dressed up in clothes of royalty. That was his original state until he rebelled.

There was party and merry making. I hope he did not eat himself to stupor because that was the first time in a long time he saw good food in abundance. He was free to eat whatever he wanted and to give away to his erstwhile neighbors. His life was turned around. He had passed through the school of life phases and now in a position to decide which of them was better. An African adage says, "a woman who has married two or more husbands knows which of them is better...probably the one she kicked out, her ex".

Until the son came back home to reconcile with his father, hired servants were far better than he. They had more than enough, and to spare. The difference is that they remained submissive to the authority of their master, were hardworking and responsible. Therefore all their needs were met. Until sons understand and stay in the place of sonship, they are no better than slaves, and do lack in the midst of plenty. Genuine freedom comes by coming back under the covering of the father. Is your father waiting for your return home? For how long would you keep him waiting? Grace always has a window period.

CHAPTER 10

THE ISSUES OF LIFE

Scripture talks about the woman with an issue of blood. The life of every living thing is in the blood. A woman loosing blood looses life, especially when it goes beyond what is common among women, according to the seasons of life. Without retelling the story over and again, this woman had spent all she had going from one doctor to the other.

At first, she would have kept it a secret to avoid embarrassment. She certainly avoided every public event and gatherings. Are you experiencing such a situation, or do you know anybody in such a precarious situation? May the Lord meet you at the point of your need in the name of Jesus. I speak PEACE to every issue in your life. Receive freedom from the Lord concerning that matter that has kept you bowed down for so long. Whatever issue you have, may the God of ultimate freedom deliver you according to your faith.

Eventually this woman would have told her close friends and relations. They would have prayed with her, fasted, diagnosed it themselves, speculated this or that. She would have sought help both within and out of state. It is so frustrating. She would have spent some time thinking about how it came about, what she did or did not do etc. When you find yourself in a situation, you discover that you are not as smart as you thought, not as strong as you thought and not as knowledgeable as you thought. In fact, you become stupid. If care is not taken, you may even lose your self-confidence.

By the time the woman had gone everywhere and spent all her substances in a period of about twelve years, she probably gave up and thought it would end in eternity. Maybe that is how God wants it. Maybe that is her luck. Maybe God is judging her for the sins of her youth, or of her forefathers. Maybe it is her roommate in college who is bewitching her. What if it was her ex-boy friend or husband?

You think now, this cannot be me. Many of us have this kind of issues. It may not be an issue of blood, but it sure is an issue. You need freedom, and no other freedom matters until the freedom from this issue becomes a reality. Little wonder this woman defied every shame and pushed through the multitude in an attempt to gain freedom. It takes a lot of gut to despise shame. "Whatever the hen is pursuing in the rain is very important to it". "If you hide a sickness because you are ashamed, then get ready for your funeral". It is the will of God for us to come "all ye that labor and are heavy laden, and get rest, for His burden is light and His yoke easy". In addition, we will find rest for our soul.

INFORMATION IS KEY

"I will walk about in freedom, for I have sought out your precepts" Psalm 119:45

David discovered what many of us are ignorant of today. Wherewith shall a young man cleanse his way? By taking heed thereto according to thy word; Ps 119:9. Taking heed means diligently seeking after. It does not in any way imply doing it your own way, or taking his precepts for-granted. Rather, it means learning his commandments and keeping them (vs. 10). It requires studying His word and saturating your mind with them. "…that you may not sin against Him" (vs 11).

The precepts and statutes of God are taught by God himself to those who diligently seek Him. We need Him to teach us and He teaches in His own way. His ordinances require that we come up to His frequency, and that costs us something. We cannot declare His ordinances unless He first teaches us His statutes. As we meditate on His precepts, and delight ourselves in His statutes, and forget not His word, then will we rejoice in His testimonies and He will guide us in the way of everlasting freedom. That is the ideal freedom.

Freedom from affliction comes by keeping the commandments and laws of the Lord (Psalm 119:153). His laws are for our benefit. Who doesn't like benefits? The ordinances of God keep us in the way of righteousness and righteousness exalts a nation. In keeping his ordinances, there is freedom. To embrace freedom and enjoy the fruits, a nation must embrace the ordinances of God. The founding fathers of the United States understand this. "In God we trust" is as relevant today as it was then. When they signed the declaration of independence, they challenged the super power of the day to do his worst. They invited the anger and subsequent punishment adequate for a "treasonable felony".

It is better to trust in the Lord, than to trust in chariots and horses. When we refuse to dwell in His secret place and abide under his shadow, we expose ourselves to the elements and the deluge could be our portion. It was gallantry to sign the dotted lines that declared independence for us, howbeit with shaky hands but not shaky minds. Freedom is a virtue worthy of pursuing at all costs that men were ready, even to lose their lives. There is no freedom anywhere that was not bought with human blood. They had to trust in God to go against the tide. When you trust in God and God is all you got, you got all you need.

In scripture we see Israel going for battles with great nations, and coming home victorious. Why? The horse could be ready for battle, but victory is of the Lord. Faith in God, is more powerful than ammunitions. Relevant to this is the question, "Do we trust in God today as our fathers did?" As an individual, a family, a community or a nation, can we sincerely say "In God We Trust"?

HISTORY REPEATS ITSELF

If we have not indentified something or a course for which we are willing even to die, we probably have not figured out the purpose of our very existence. History is replete with people who died for what they believed: what a good way to die! Paul the apostle puts it in a very clear language "to live is Christ and to die is gain (Phil 1:21)". What is he talking about? To die is gain? Did he want to die young? I don't think so.

Did he mean we should all aspire to die for the gain in death? Not precisely. I think the great apostle got to the point in his ministry that he knew that death was a necessary end that would come when it would. For everybody will go the way of all men, someday. We may not know when and how it will come, because it is already appointed. Unfortunately, it is not the appointment you can easily vote and change as you like. "For it is appointed unto man once to die, after which, the judgment (Heb. 9:27).

Paul knew the natural pathway, but his faith, ministry, and vocation exposed him to perils daily. People who could not stand the gospel were eager to kill him, and he was not at home also with false brethren who thought he was pushing the faith too far. They are like the Egyptians who didn't mind Israel going to worship their God in the wilderness after the plagues, but didn't want them to go far. So long as you practice religion, but still follow the trends, they will be your friends. I leave you to answer Peters question "shall we obey men rather than God?" Shall we seek the approval of men and despise God's?

Some people think it is sacrilege to preach what you believe. Everything you believe to be wrong, somebody somewhere does not see anything wrong with it. If you preach morality for example, immoral people would not allow you within their circles because you condemn what they find pleasurable. When Paul was preaching Christ and the crucifixion/resurrection of Christ his redeemer, some of the people wondered what the "babbler" was talking about. They threw him in jail after jail, accusing him of breaking the law, of civil disobedience etc. He was tried before Agrippa (who almost became a Christian just by listening to Paul speak). Also Felix the governor could not find any evidence to convict Paul of the people's accusations.

"For the preaching of the cross is to them that perish foolishness, but to those who are being saved, it is the power of God (1Cor.1:18). Paul knew his past and his future. He was quite aware of the differences. He knew what happened to him and how his conversion was by the finger of God. He knew his God and had a personal experience of what He could do. He needed no man to approve of him or to commission his assignment. He responded to it in a way that vividly expressed his understanding of the reason for which he still lived. He knew he would go the way of all men the day he finished his assignment, and that a great reward awaited him yonder.

What more did he know? That he needed to finish his work to his master's satisfaction to get the crown of glory. So he determined that "No man engaged in a military assignment entangles himself with civilian affairs (2 Tim. 2:4). He rose up to the call of duty with a zeal second to none, generated from within. He laid his hands on the plough and would not look back. He had discovered his assignment and nothing else was important. His assignment consumed him. He knew he would die yet he continued, because even that was beneficial. When you get to that point where you are ready to die for your assignment, then you have started living for your assignment. This is the best way to live a life of freedom. Otherwise, you will not find fulfillment in life and ministry.

Your freedom begins with that discovery and willingness to do what is not common and popular in your bid to fulfill your calling. The problem you were created to solve will so infuriate you that everything else is not strong enough to deter you.

At first, you may appear foolish to people that care about you and those you care about. You may even try to suppress the push from within you to take a stand for or against whatever it is because taking that stand would obviously not win the vote of the day. Vote? In my generation, as in the days of Paul, standing up to stand out for your assignment is not likely going to win the vote of the day. That's not what you want to hear, right?

For example, let's assume that your assignment is to liberate a people from the tyranny of another. When you take that stance, you will be cajoled, kidnapped, jailed etc. You will probably become notorious, before (in rare cases) becoming popular. You must learn against all odds to be focused on your assignment in the midst of diverse distractions. Greatness comes in being able to go all the way, regardless. You must see what nobody is seeing, and must not be afraid to stand alone.

Men are going to gang up against you, using whatever means available to stop you. They would find faults in what you say and what you do, as in what you did not say or do. If you pray four hours a day, they would enact laws against praying four hours a day so as to get you for breaking the law. You will have to wage wars within, trying to do what is popular versus what is penitent. If you want to be at peace with men by doing what they would approve, you will not be at peace with yourself and your conscience. What greater bondage is there than to be in prison within you. Paul the apostle knew that our soul rests only when it finds rest in Christ.

CHAPTER 11

THE PHILOSPHY OF FREEDOM

FREEDOM IS NOT A PLACE

There is no place left without people actively and passively desiring and seeking, if not fighting for freedom, one way or another. It could be political freedom, economic freedom, or any kind of freedom for that matter. This has, in history, led to all kinds of wars, civil unrests and revolutions. When people demonstrate in the streets, often times it is because they believe that what is legitimately theirs is being denied, diverted or usurped. Sometime, it may just be delayed, and human beings have a natural way of wanting what is theirs "now"…a kind of "it is my money, and I want it now".

In the debates on issues around freedom, there are always many players. One of the things that fuel the temptation to deny freedom is self interest, the essence of economics. But more than demand and supply, there is greed in the heart of men. Adam Smith argued that it is not because the cloth designer cares so much about naked people that he made clothes, rather it is the money he would make from selling them that motivates him, so is the car designer.

Nature made man a package. This package has good things and bad, and in that package is a tendency to be greedy. The natural man has this tendency, especially if there are not enough strong societal institutions set up to check man's excesses.

Think about people who are poor in rich countries. One of the reasons the United States is a free country is that she takes care of her poor citizens and respects the rights and voices of her masses. The US is one of the countries where the poor have voices, even if they have merely poor voices. Oh, how I wish the rest of the world would emulate the US.

Some may argue that the rich have more voices than the poor, and I do agree; but at least the poor have voices and rights. The voices of the poor keep the rich from oppressing the poor with impunity. That is why an employer cannot just wake up one day and fire someone just because he did not feel good that day. The law will hold him to accounts.

Back to the poor who live in rich countries with rich corrupt legacies. It used to be that a man could say whatever he wanted about the governor of his state while seated in his house and no one bothered him. Today in those states, you dare not talk anyhow else you will be kidnapped. You criticize the government and challenge injustice at your peril. It has got so bad that at a bus stop, you could actually see a young lady being robbed of her jewelry and purse, yet the rest of the people will keep quiet or even look away to the other direction under the guise of "minding their own business". The young lady could cry all she wants and call for help all she wants and nobody comes to her rescue. Those are societies robbed of neighborhood and the spirit of community. Impunity in the high and low places is the order of the day, and the rule of law is disregarded.

It used to be that thieves came by night, sneaked in unnoticed and masked. If need be, they wait for the people to travel or be gone for some event so they can break in and steal whatever they find. Nowadays, they write you letters or even send you text messages giving you advanced notice of their intended visitation. At first it would sound like a joke, but then they show up.

God will have to deliver you by a special angel if you don't have enough money to meet their unnecessarily high, irrational and irresponsible demands. Don't even ask me where the police and other law enforcement agents would be when things like these happen. It actually does appear as if they work together with the police to carry out their nefarious activities.

The above examples only show that people living in those places are in urgent need of freedom – freedom from the activities of evil men, who come in bandits and evil men who choose to do nothing to protect the invalid or the less privileged. In "Unguarded Moments", we talked about wives who are assaulted by husbands, even on daily basis, and nothing happens. Every place something like that happens and somebody can only cry without having any ideas of what to do or who to call for help, somebody is in need of freedom. The need for freedom is ubiquitous. Freedom is not a place. Otherwise, I want to go and live there.

FREEDOM IS A STATE

Freedom is a state, not necessarily a physical state like Anambra State, the state of Texas, etc. It is a mental state and knows no geographical boundaries although its exercise in practice could be geographically limited. You are not free because you think you are free, but you cannot be free unless you first think and accept in your mind that you can be free. It does not necessarily matter where you are, you can be free. Therefore, freedom is not a place that you want to go, just like a place where you are cannot guarantee you of freedom the way you think of the concept but you can choose to live in the state of freedom even in an un-free place.

The greatest enemy of freedom and obstacle to its ultimate attainment is not the place where you are or what you do, have or have not become; it is your failure to believe that you can be free where you are. Like many of the pursuits and battles of life, until your mind can perceive it and accommodate it, your eyes cannot see it and your hands cannot touch it. That is why it is said that the greatest nation on the face of the earth is imagination: which I define as the state of your mind.

When you tell somebody something that blows their mind, something they have neither heard nor witnessed before and something they never thought is possible; they rhetorically ask the next person, "Can you imagine that?" That is a question, sometimes of doubt, unbelief and lack of faith. In secular terms, we call it the power of imagination; in Christian terms we call it the power of faith. You need faith, and imagination to take hold of freedom, however you define it.

CHAPTER 12

FAITH AND FREEDOM

FAITH IS NOW

In the twelfth chapter of Hebrews, the Bible talks about the heroes of faith. Before we look at scriptures, let us consider this. A young man wanted to get a job as a janitor in one of the big companies in a town but they would not employ him because he had a "record" from his teenage years of juvenile delinquencies. Such "records" are offshoots of the freedom madness of this generation especially when teenagers despise counsel and instruction, rebuke and corrections. They get into troubles that follow them, perhaps for the rest of what remains of their lives. When we make decisions and choices, we attract consequences that would linger sometime for years or a lifetime, if not trans-generationally. Freedom is not a license to live recklessly.

This young man approached certain manager to see if he would help him. As they spoke, the manager realized this young man wanted to be useful but was being hunted by his past. He desperately needed freedom from the grip of his past. The manager introduced the idea of going back to school as one of the ways to outrun his past. At first, the young man didn't think he was college material, besides, he thought it would take lots of years to graduate with something meaningful. People want freedom, now – a kind of fire brigade approach. The manager asked him what he considered "something meaningful" and he said, "like what you do". The manager laughed hilariously.

He wanted to be like the manager but he was not willing to commit several years to college like the manager did. Eventually the manager was able to convince him to go to college. They agreed he had to start somewhere and take it one step at a time, with a mind set on the final destination. A couple of months later, he came back to meet the manager smiling as he boldly displayed the inscription on his college vest. He had been accepted in a nearby college and was happily taking classes, so he came to give the manager situation report. The manager congratulated him and assured him that a journey to the state of freedom from janitorial work had begun. The way to start enjoying freedom is to do now that which will give you freedom tomorrow.

As a graduate student in the UK, I worked in a warehouse loading trucks with merchandise. My supervisors did not have high school diplomas, even though I already had a pharmacy degree and two master's degrees. I was already enrolled in a doctorate degree and still working in the warehouse. What my colleagues in the warehouse did not know was that I was not competing with them. There was an advertisement for a team leader and all the people were applying, I didn't mind them. Most of them were buying good cars, houses etc and making their careers, but I knew freedom for me was something that was not available in the warehouse. I was pursuing my doctorate in public health, and at the same time pursuing my pharmacy licensing exams in the United States. I still drove my old car.

One day my manager changed my schedule without notice, claiming it was purely a business need. I tried in vain to get him to reason with me, but he would not. Then I excused myself and pulled up my webpage on the school website, as I explained that I was a research student and his schedule was going to get in the way of my research He was shocked.

He didn't understand what I was doing in the warehouse. He didn't know how to act. Still he didn't change my schedule. So I took off my high visibility vest, and my helmet, gave them to him and walked away. That was the last time I worked in a warehouse. Fortunately, I cannot wait to visit again to see how many of them are still in the warehouse loading and off-loading trucks. Looking back now, I wonder how I survived those days of hard labor. My freedom was possible today because I did something then that my colleagues at the warehouse would not and could not do. In that economic sense, my freedom tomorrow depends on what I do today. The seed we sow today determines the fruit we harvest tomorrow.

I worked full time in the classroom and full time in the warehouse.

COUNT THE COST

Jesus could not have saved the world from eternal death without dying himself. Martin Luther King Jnr could not have made any remarkable achievement if he was afraid to be put to death in his prime. There are costs associated with everything, it doesn't matter if you got it free – someone somewhere somehow paid for it. Think about it. If you got a free ticket to go cruising to Hawaii, somebody paid for it. If you ate lunch at K-bob or MrBiggs, somebody paid for it. Don't you dare take the fact that you did not pay for it for-granted, it came from the pocket maybe of a friend, a dad or a good Samaritan.

Growing up in Africa, I had such good parents that I took a lot of things for-granted. Although we were not rich, my dad earned our respect because he was always there for us and provided what we needed, not what we wanted, because he couldn't afford to buy a chopper bicycle for us. Today at 75 years old and retired, he is happy that his children are doing well.

He counted the cost, and provided us with education and the encouragement to go further. Then he did not hang out with his mates in the bar or pub to drink and party. He knew that his greatest gift to his children was going to cost him something, and it did. He didn't buy a car for himself, but now he can drive if he wants to. He didn't travel a lot then, now he can come to the United States to hang out with his grand children. His efforts pay off, and now he is free to enjoy his retirement however he wants. Guess what? His contemporaries who could not make the sacrifices he made then are jealous of him today.

THE IMPORTANCE OF FAITH 2Pet.1:1-10

Faith is so important in life that without it you cannot achieve anything, not even freedom. To a Christian, it is so vital that even Christianity itself is referred to as "the faith". Without faith, it is impossible to please God (Heb 11:6) for he that must come to God or call on Him must first believe that He is able and willing to reward those that diligently seek Him.

You cannot seek God diligently unless you believe He is and He has something you so desperately need. There is a difference between seeking God casually and seeking him diligently. Many of us seek Him casually, especially when it appears everything is going fine, until things go wrong. What if we seek him as diligently everyday as we do when things go wrong?

A four year old Sunday school girl once said that God is fake because she has never seen Him even though mummy says to pray to God. Over time, the child began to learn to believe and to trust in God as she observed her parents pray and acknowledge God in all their ways. It was of paramount importance that the parents took time to lead the little inquisitive mind in the right direction as far as her belief and faith in God is concerned. That is parenting. But how could the parents direct the four year old if they at forty-four are still trying to figure out if God actually exists or not? If you find yourself in such a situation, I will be glad to point you in the right direction.

Before we take a journey with Apostle Peter on the subject of "add to your faith" in Chapter 13, why do we need to add anything else to our faith? Does it mean that faith in itself is not enough? How does faith relate to the subject of freedom? What do I need to add and how? Keep those questions going in your mind as we try to address them in this and the next chapter.

FAITH IS BELIEF ACCOMPANIED BY ACTION. Like we earlier implied, it takes faith to be a Christian. Many of us have not seen God or Jesus, yet we believe He came in the form of man, and died for our salvation. The Bible tells us, and we believe that there is no other name under heaven given among men by which we must be saved. That is the elemental faith…the faith that saves. If the faith that drew you to salvation is enough to sustain you on your journey through the thick and thin, then you wouldn't need to add anything to it. I am convinced that Peter argues that you need much more than just believing that Jesus is Lord to live a victorious Christian life.

I choose to define faith as believing and behaving – a belief that leads to a change in behavior. It is belief (in our heart) that leads to a change, both in our confession (utterances) and profession (actions). Therefore faith is active and dynamic. Dynamic faith is productive and productive faith is dynamic. If your faith is not dynamic, it is faithless.

Of what use is a car that cannot move? The woman with the issue of blood had faith, and her faith got her on her feet to travel in the direction where she would meet and touch Jesus at the helm of His garment. If she had faith and sat down in her house afraid of the jeer of the multitude, Jesus would have probably passed bye and she would have probably died with her issue. She had the freedom of choice, and the choice she made got her the freedom she so desperately needed – from the issue of blood.

Abram believed God in his heart and he left his kindred in obedience to God and followed as God led him. He believed that God exists, and that God is not just real but realistic. He trusted that God was leading him to a place better than the Ur of the Chaldeans. His belief travelled from his heart to his feet and arms, as he packed his belongings, commanded his servants, saddled the asses and bid his kinfolks farewell. It was a long nomadic life and experience, yet he did not change his mind nor did he regret that initial obedience. One obedience sustained the other and the other, until his descendants inherited the Promised Land years after he had died.

Abram, where are you going with your whole possession? To a place God will show me. Are you kidding? What is the name of the place? I don't know? You don't know where He is leading you? Yes. Are you out of your mind? Does it make sense to you? Can you listen to yourself Abram? When did you become lunatic? That God of yours must be unreasonable too. Can you stretch this conversation by your imagination and see the kind of things that must have gone on in the minds of Abram's ungodly kinsmen. Have you experienced a thing like that before? If not, it is either you are so blessed to be surrounded only by people who believe in God and appreciate His acts, or your Christianity is such a secret or unreal that people around you can even swear by their gods you are neither a Christian nor do you understand Christianity.

Abram had faith in God that even his kinsmen who do not believe in God saw the manifestation of his faith. He didn't know where he was going yet he kept going. The instruction to leave didn't make sense to men, but God's instruction doesn't have to make sense to men because men do not operate at the frequency that God does. God does not have to align himself to our agenda, we must figure out how to partner with God in what He is doing.

Moreover, we don't follow God with our head, we follow Him with our heart. If you follow God with your head, you will stumble over and again, else your head will blow open. If man could figure God out with his head, the universe would have been different because man would have carried out reverse engineering on everything that God has put in place. With all our knowledge, there is a limitation which makes us human, and the infiniteness of God which makes Him divine. The freedom to figure God out is not given to man.

Abraham understood this, so he followed God even though he did not know where he was going. He trusted that God knew what He was doing. He knew that when God leads you, he feeds you. He does not lead anyone but beside still waters like a shepherd leads his flock. As God leads you He trims you; and He leads you in the path of everlasting peace. His leadings guarantee great things. Again, your faith in God may demand that you do that which is unpopular and sometime unreasonable to the human mind. More seriously, it would demand that you do that which is uncomfortable to you.

If you only operate by the things that men relate with and approve of, then you will not please God because His instructions will not win the vote of the day, and you must know that from the onset of your journey with Him so you don't miss Him on the way. If you are such a person that doesn't want to offend anybody, doesn't want people to say bad things about you, and doesn't want to be seen standing up when others are sitting down, you will never be outstanding in your walk with God. When everybody else is sitting down, your faith in God may demand that you stand up to stand out. What people say is not always important in the business of the kingdom.

Abram stood up for God and stood out from the crowd. He had faith…what most of us are still struggling with. Do you have faith enough in God to trust Him with your life and future? Did you just say 'Yes"? Many of us would say yes even though we sometime doubt if our faith is big enough to move any mountains…maybe not even as big as a mustard seed. How miserable a faith?

His name was Eric Liddell, a Scottish Olympic champion at the 1924 Olympic Games who refused to run on a Sunday because it was against his belief. It didn't matter that the whole world thought otherwise, even Christians that belong to the same church thought he could have run and dedicate the race to God, but Eric was alone and didn't bother. The press made mockery, and derogatory comments about him but he stood his ground. Incidentally, he competed in the race that was not scheduled on a Sunday, which was not the race he was good at, but he left a record that was unbeaten for almost forty years.

While the rest of Scotland and the United Kingdom yet celebrated him, he announced that he was going off to China to become a missionary, after his father. It didn't win the vote of the day, but that is the assignment to which he dedicated the rest of his otherwise short life, so much that he died in mission field.

You are welcome to read the full account of his life and ministry in a book titled, Eric Liddell: God's Athlete by Catherine Swift. I am sure it will challenge you the way it challenged me and shook my foundations. At his death bed, all he could scribble was "Be still my soul, the Lord is on thy side" which was the song they sang at his funeral.

CHAPTER 13

THE ACCOMPLICES OF FAITH

There are seven attributes that Peter admonishes us to add to our faith…so that we will be fruitful in our service and knowledge of our Lord Jesus Christ. Of what importance to the kingdom is a Christian who is not fruitful? Is it possible to have faith yet be unfruitful? Why is it important for a Christian to be fruitful in his knowledge? What do you do to a tree that is not fruitful?

My dad planted some avocado seedlings in our compound in Nigeria back in the 80s. Over time, some of them grew and began to bear fruits. Oh, we enjoyed those fruits.

There was one of them that refused to bear fruit. We didn't know if it was diseased, or genetically unfortunate. At some point, my dad began to apply manure, fertilizer and all that, to give it added attention to see if it would bear fruit, yet to no avail. One year, after every effort had been made to help it be useful, it was cut off and in its place, another planted.

Is that not what happens to us when we refuse to be fruitful? To avoid a situation like this, Peter admonishes us, towards the end of his life, to add to our faith …

VIRTUE: To faith, add virtue. This is another word for courage. Adding virtue to your faith means taking a stand for God and being strong and courageous. There are many people who are Christians, and have faith but are not courageous to take a stand for God or godliness. There are situations when it is not popular to take a stand for God, at such times courage is needed.

In this generation when even governments make policies that are at variance with the Christian faith, we need Christians who would stand for the word of God and defend the faith.

Joshua was to lead the Israelites into the land of Canaan, he needed to be courageous, so as to fight the good fight of faith. Freedom was going to remain an illusion unless they acted courageously. When you see the children of Anak in the land, you would know that the ten spies, who did not have good reports, were only stating the facts, devoid of faith. That was their offence.

KNOWLEDGE: To virtue, add knowledge. Our knowledge of God and the word of God must keep increasing, so is our knowledge of what is going on in the society. This is possible through study… "to show yourself approved unto God, a workman that needs not to be ashamed, rightly dividing the word of truth". It is not enough to be courageous and to take a stand for God, we need to arm ourselves with knowledge. Knowledge is power, and it is key. When Jesus was tempted by the devil, he armed himself with a good knowledge of the word "it is written". How many people who have faith in God have a working and reliable knowledge of the word and its application in real life situations?

Are we not free to study the word? It appears that in countries where Christians are persecuted, they tend to be more dedicated to their faith. Those who are free to do whatever they want with the Bible and the word of God abandon it for other things. Even Jesus was knowledgeable in political and civil matters and current affairs. Esther and Nehemiah could not have achieved much if they did not have a working knowledge of the times and the seasons.

TEMPERANCE: To knowledge, add temperance. This is another word for self-control. A Christian who cannot control himself will deny the faith he claims to have. Because we are still in the world, and in the flesh, there are many things that are not sinful, yet a Christian must be careful how he accepts them, and how he allows them. We are free to do things, but we must not use our freedom as an occasion for lasciviousness. It is not everything your eyes see and like that we should have. It is not everything that you can afford that you must buy. There are events that will arise if you do not exercise self-control, you will deny the faith and set yourself up for ridicule.

PATIENCE: To temperance, add patience. Patience is very important in the life of a Christian, especially when things don't go as we planned. In the journey through life, divergent voices would speak to you when you are taking a stand for God. If you listen to the voice of the devil to go back to the world, then you will lose out of the promises of God, both in this life and in the life to come.

Some people want patience right now. Others are not patient with God even in the exercise of their faith. Patience is the oil with which relationships are lubricated. Abraham was a man of faith, and he excelled in patience. Isaac was also patient. Sometime, there is a long lag time between the promise and its manifestation...patience is needed. In your struggle for freedom, you will have to endure hardship as a good soldier.

GODLINESS: To patience, add godliness. Godliness speaks of living for God. It is living your life to the glory of God alone. It requires diligence in doing things that will glorify God. A godly person is conscious of what he does and what image it projects. In Christian living, we have freedom, but not to live our lives anyhow.

The early apostles of Jesus were living their lives in the community, going about their businesses, exhibiting characters that depicted Christ and the people called them Christians. It was not a fashionable title then as it is now, but it shows that they were different.

In our generation, everybody claims to be a Christian yet there is no difference between us and the world. In fact, the church is increasingly becoming more worldly than the world…which is unfortunate. We crucify Christ time and again by living ungodly lives and we think it doesn't matter. We have modernized Christianity in our bid to make God conform to our desires and line up with our wishes. We want to be celebrated both by Christians and non-Christians, and we call it political correctness.

We want to make everybody happy, even by the messages we preach from the pulpit, and in the process we lose God in the congregation. It used to be that the message of the cross was to them that perish foolishness, but now we want to mellow down a little so that they don't call us fanatics. What has become of the old time religion? Is that part of the claim to freedom? Do we have freedom to adulterate Christianity?

BROTHERLY KINDNESS: To godliness, add brotherly kindness. This means we need to show kindness to the brethren. Abraham readily comes to mind each time we talk about brotherly kindness. We know him as a man of faith, but he exemplifies brotherly kindness. God called him out of his kindred, and he took Lot along with him. Lot became greedy and wouldn't remember how he came to become prosperous, and quickly chose to go the way that ultimately led to Sodom. He met with calamity yet Abraham risked his life and that of his men to fight for Lot, his nephew.

Even when there was a quarrel between Abraham's servants and Lot's servants, Abraham pleaded for peace, noting that "we are brethren". Lot thought he had the freedom to choose, so he chose the green pastures to the east.

Brotherly kindness demands that we give people second chances. God is a God of second chances, and sometimes he gives us second chances again and again. Are there couples who claim to be godly, yet they have kept a log of offences that are ten years old? Sometimes we claim that we are brought up to keep records, so we maintain a diary for offences. Unfortunately, if we kept diary of good things as much as we keep diary of offences, the world would be a better place. Let brotherly kindness reign in our hearts…we have the freedom to make it happen.

LOVE: To brotherly kindness, add love. Love is the greatest of all. It covers a multitude of sin. In his epistle to the Corinthians church, Paul wrote extensively on the importance of love. If we have faith, patience, godliness, brotherly kindness, self control, knowledge, but no love, we have nothing. God has all of these attributes, but the only thing that motivated him to save mankind is love.

"For God so loved the world that he gave His only begotten son". Then he made a provision for us, "that whosoever will believe in him will not perish, but will have everlasting life". He gave us options, showed us the way of escape, and now it is up to us to choose life that we may live. That is freedom of choice at its peak.

When you discover the need, and make that choice, and Jesus sets you free, then are you free indeed. "For He did not come to condemn the world, but that the world through Him might be saved". This is the free gift of God to mankind, and the best gift ever given, yet the world has refused to accept it. Every other discussion on freedom begins after this freedom has become a reality in our lives.

CHAPTER 14

THE RIGHT SIDE OF HISTORY

FOR US OR FOR OUR ADVERSARIES (Josh 5:13-15)

Israel, under the leadership of Joshua was free to choose whether to follow and obey God, or to do their own bidding. When you choose to do your own bidding, it wouldn't be long before you outbid yourself. The idea of circumcision was not any man's, but God's. I have no doubts that it was not an exercise to which any grown up man would look forward in excitement, neither in the days of Joshua nor in my days.

Joshua had made an end of circumcising the second generation of the people at Gilgal according to the commandment of God (Josh 4:9) and the Lord had rolled away the reproach of Egypt from among them. All Israel still camped at Gilgal and kept the Passover, yet another directive not of human idea.

Israel again was free from the dictates of a Pharaoh, but not free from the dictates of God. Until they ate the first fruit in the land of Canaan, manna still fell and God still fed them with quail. So His demands on the people were for their benefits. Everything God needs to be God is already in Him, whether we line up with Him or not.

It may, perhaps help for us to say that Israel prospered under the leadership of Joshua. Everywhere we see Joshua mentioned in scripture, he comes across as a man of faith and obedience. In Exod.17:9-10, he obeyed the commandments of Moses the servant of God. When they spied out the land of Canaan, it was him and Caleb that believed God and wanted to go up immediately to possess the land. The idea excited him, and that excitement probably made him to excel. Almost forty years after when he was called upon to succeed Moses, he obeyed the call (Josh 1:5-11). He led them into the historic Promised Land. All the days of Joshua, Israel served the Lord (Josh 24:31) and by the time of his death, Joshua was known simply as "the servant of the Lord" (Judges 2:7-8). Can you beat that?

We consider him exceptional leader today, not because he was the most intelligent, most powerful, most handsome etc, but because he was an obedient servant. He was careful not to depart from the commandments of the Lord, so he prospered and had good success as Moses assured him. At your death, if God and men would say of you "he was a servant of God", you have the greatest title there is. The only thing that will guarantee that is obedience to the word of God you already know.

As Joshua saw this man by Jericho with his sword drawn in his hand as a soldier ready for war, he, being a very courageous leader went forth and stood before him to inquire about his mission. Are you for us or for our enemies? Have you come for peace or pieces?

I am neither for you nor for your enemies, it seems the man had implied, or better put, the question was begged. "No, but as the commander of the army of the Lord I have now come (vs 14). Obviously this guy was a stranger, with a strange mission it appeared. Joshua would probably have asked more questions if he had time and opportunity. One of those questions would have been "what do you want?"

I learnt not to ask somebody "What do you want?" and not risk being misunderstood when I moved to the United States and worked as an intern. At that time, many of my clients struggled with my Africanized British accent and I also struggled with some of the southern accents as well.

A lady rang the pharmacy and this zealous intern was on the other side of the phone. 'What do you want?' caused a big quarrel. She was so mad. "What do you mean by what do you want?" she asked as she demanded to speak to somebody else "who knew what was going on". I apologized profusely because I did not mean any disrespect or offences. Well, I have not asked that question again in five years.

Joshua had the freedom to have dispatched some of his men to interrogate this stranger. If a man stood before you in that setting with sword drawn, the first impression is that he is ready for war. If you see a man in your house with his gun in his hand standing on a land that you contend with somebody, you will quickly reach for your ammunition. He was free to assume, but he would have assumed wrongly and probably suffered for it. Assumption is a deadly master. It can end your life and mess up your destiny. What you say to a stranger is important, and how you say it is also important. We need to be careful how we approach and treat strangers, whether they have swords in their hands or nothing at all.

Are you an ally or an adversary? Why did he show up bodily and unannounced? Joshua needed to know things that no man could have told him, but God could have told him in a dream. Yes, but the appearance of the commander in physical form made it more remarkable. Joshua did not forget that experience for the rest of his life.In our freedom to choose and to do, we need to know that God is still in charge and in control of the affairs of man.

The ground upon which he stood was holy but Joshua knew it not. Why didn't he know that? How could he have known? He needed a re-assurance that God was still involved and interested in the affairs of Israel, and that greater are they with them than they with the enemies. He needed to gird his loins and advance as the Lord directs without any fear. Moreover, he was reminded that victory is of the Lord.

God does not need to line up with our agenda, we need to line up with the agenda of God. If you are not careful, you fight the wrong person and the wrong battle in your claim to freedom. Joshua could have started a battle he would never have won. How many times do we fight such battles?

The stranger at your door could be God-sent to give you a lifetime encounter and to move you to the next level of your life and ministry. How many people have been blessed with such an angelic visitation? How many times in his lifetime did Joshua experience such a visit? Why did he have to remove his sandals from off his feet?

It was not an ordinary angel that visited Joshua at Jericho, it was God incarnate. How do I know that? He did not stop Joshua from bowing down to worship him. Angels are fellow servants, and they don't let you worship them. Only God deserves our worship. Also, He said to Joshua, "the ground where you stand is holy". When a holy God shows up, the place is made holy by his presence. In the days of the Levitical priests, they were commanded to remove their sandals when they serve in the priest's office at the holy place because the presence of God makes the temple holy.

Joshua was in the place of his assignment taking care of business as usual. Jericho was before them – the city was already shut from everybody – no entry, no exit. The city walls were fortified and their security second to none. Something had to happen. Joshua and all Israel must fight and overcome Jericho, but how is that conquest going to work out?

The Lord shows up with his sword in his hand. He appeared as the captain of the hosts of the Lord's army. Joshua had to relinquish his authority and submit to the authority of God wholly and entirely. To exercise authority, you must submit to authority. To be free, you must be compliant with directives. So as soon as Joshua fell and worshipped, and asked what the Lord wants him to do, he was commanded to remove his sandals. He obeyed without hesitation.

The Relevance of Sandals

Sandals are barriers from the elements. They provide comfort and make us sure-feeted. They could be signs of authority as in the case of Boaz. When one removed his sandal, he yielded his right, his authority.

In the presence of God, you make yourself vulnerable. It is a mark of total yielding - total surrender to his authority over you – a mark of respect and a sign of allegiance. Joshua was totally surrendered to the Lord and the Lord himself led the war. Have you ever heard of such a strategy as the strategy that defeated Jericho? They walked round the city once a day and seven times on the seventh day and everybody screamed. Fortified city walls came tumbling down. How do you explain that to an engineer or an architect? The host of the armies of the Lord led the war with his drawn sword.

When you walk with God in obedience, He shows up at those moments when you cannot handle a given situation. There is no way Joshua could have defeated Jericho unaided. The Lord had to show up in person, and would not even send an angel. Joshua had freedom of choice and he chose to obey God explicitly. When Israel thought they defeated Jericho and so could take on Ai, look at the defeat they suffered.

The presence of Jehovah made the difference between winning a war and losing a battle. The strategy that wins every war is the Lord's strategy. You are free to abandon the Lord's directives, and of course free to suffer the consequences of operating without His leading.

What if Joshua refused to remove his sandals and still expected to win the war with Jericho or Ai? The Lord's sword is always two-edged. You want to be on the Lord's side in the day of his anger. He honors those that honor Him. He strengthens His own and expects them to walk according to His precepts. Isn't it interesting that as soon as He had commanded Joshua to remove his sandals, the Bible did not talk about anything else other than the destruction of Jericho. That's what the Lord came to do.

On the Jericho side of things, they had thought they were free from external aggression by reason of their fortified city walls...they were wrong. A man is not saved by the fortification of his fences. When the Lord shows up with His sword in His hands, the gates lift up their heads in honor of the king of kings and the walls fell down to worship Him. As Joshua fell down to worship, so did the walls and the Israelites marched in and slaughtered the people of Jericho by the finger of God.

CHAPTER 15

THE PLACE OF SERENDIPITY

FREEDOM BY SERENDIPITY 2 Kings 6:24-7:3

It will be helpful for the reader to look at this bible passage for a detailed account of what happened. There was famine in the land of Samaria and the city was besieged by the Syrians. The gates of the city were locked that nobody went in or went out. The famine was so severe that people bought animal dung to eat, and until they became cannibals. There was no food anywhere.

In those days, lepers were ostracized from the rest of the people. There were these four lepers at the gate – outside. Their people had kicked them out of the city because of their situation. Apparently they were leprous on their skin but not leprous on their minds. They were not free to mix with the people, but they were free to stretch their imaginations, and they did.

Certain attributes are worthy of note about these men.

(1). They were Samarians with blemishes. The fact that they had leprosy did not change who they were…they still identified with their people. Who could have predicted that they would be useful to humanity in their diseased state? But God had an agenda. The church must learn to stop killing her wounded soldiers. We must be slow to write people off, assuming they are good for nothing. This passage amply demonstrates that the ways of God are different from ours, and everybody can be useful. I believe all scriptures are given to us by the inspiration of the Holy Spirit, and are profitable for teaching.

(2) The four lepers had leprosy in their body but not in their mind and spirit; the people inside the city who put them out probably had leprosy in their minds and spirit. Leprosy is a disease of insensitivity. If you have leprosy in your body, your nerve cells are dead and you don't feel sensations anymore. You become insensitive in that part of the body to pain, heat, cold, etc. When you have leprosy in your mind, you lose sensitivity to the voice of God, to the move of God and to the agenda of God. The church has a pandemic of leprosy.

There are too many issues with which the people contended. They all had a common concern at this point in time...how to go beyond the city gate in search of food in the midst of unimaginable famine. The problem of the Syrians defied them, both the clean and the leprous. Nobody was free to go anywhere, not even the king. Everyone was afraid of death, either from the Syrians or from the famine. Those who were separated by leprosy were united in the need for freedom from the dual jeopardy of the day.

(3) The four lepers were outside the gates of the city, exposed to the elements. Their people did not care so much for them about possible harm from the enemies because they were leprous. Whatever happened to them was ok, after all they were lepers. They certainly felt the very first impact of the famine before the rest of the city.

The gates of the city were shut against them, possibly to die of their leprosy. They sat at the gate all day and all night, having nobody to beg alms from because nobody went in or came out of the city. Theirs was a case of multiple jeopardy – leprosy, ostracism, hunger, cold, etc. There was no hope, either of their situation or of their state. They probably stopped worrying about their leprosy and began to worry about food to eat. In any case, they were at risk of death either by hunger or by the hands of Syrian invaders.

The people inside the city were also as worried for themselves as the lepers for food, but at least they enjoyed relative security from the invaders. The siege was so fearful and the famine so intense that people began to eat their children. Even the king had no idea what to do. Everybody was apparently looking for whom to blame. Solution was nowhere in sight.

Everybody needs food, both in those days and nowadays. Subsistence is important, both to the free and the slave. Without food, how can you say you are free? You are free to work, do anything else but when it is lunch time or dinner time, you know that your productivity is going to be affected. We all need to be free from hunger. In this generation, there are people who cannot skip a meal let alone go without food for days or months. The Bible did not expressly tell us how long the siege lasted…it probably lasted several months. This is evident from the fact that even animal dung was sold for so much.

Apart from food, security is also important to man. If it was only about famine, it could have been easier to handle. The people were hungry, and afraid for the invasion of the enemy. Nobody went in, nobody went out of the city, for only-God-knows how long. Believe me, if people could eat their children it was no longer child's play. Many would have died of hunger, else how would it have been obvious to the four lepers that they would die regardless of what they did or did not do?

The man of God (Elijah) was there with the elders, apparently to seek the face of God on their predicaments. As the woman reported to the king the treachery of her friend, the king decided that the man of God must die. Why do you want to kill the man of God? If God had decided to withhold rain and food, or not to save a city, what would the prophet do?

As the emissary of the king came up to the prophet, the prophet was in the spirit and declared what was going to happen but was doubted. By this time tomorrow, food will sell for so much (next to nothing) at the gates of

Samaria. How can that be, even if God opens the windows of heaven? This was a man on whose shoulder the king leaned. That is remarkable. He must have been a very noble person. In wisdom, he must have excelled. He must have been well learned, probably the kings economic adviser. He understood the laws of nature and of economics, being very familiar with the way things work in the kingdom. He has lived long enough and been around for a while that he could as well be a consultant on the ways of God. He probably did not recon with the prophet, because he was more educated, richer and more respected in the society. He believed he had more going on than the man of God.

Even if God opens doors and windows in heaven, can this thing be? He forgot that a king is not saved by the multitude, both of his knowledge and his soldiers. He also forgot that the ways of God are quite different from ours. He did not remember that God calls those things that be not as though they were. He let his academic prowess, political wizardry and economic expertise get into his head. He thought he could figure God out because the king trusted him and relied on his know-how. He also forgot that the earth is the Lord's and the fullness thereof, the world and the people therein. He did not realize that the horse may be ready for battle, but victory is of the Lord.

How can this be? Some people are enslaved by their knowledge and understanding. Before we answer his question, let's ask Mr Adviser, how did the heaven and the earth come into existence? How did David kill Goliath with one stone? How did God spread out the sky without pillars? What is manna, and from where did quail fall to feed the Israelites in the wilderness?

How does a grain of corn germinate, grow and bear whole cob? How does a fetus develop into a baby, and how does the baby grow? When you barb your hair or clip your nails, how do they grow back up? When night falls, you retire to sleep: how do you wake up from your sleep in the morning? Mr wise man! How did the red sea part this way and that to let the Israelites pass on dry ground? How did Joseph rise from prison to prime minister over night?

There is life and safety in believing. Believe God, so shall you be established; believe his prophet so shall you prosper. "You shall surely see it with your eyes but you shall not eat of it". He probably still remained doubtful, until . . .

Why do we sit here and risk annihilation? If we stay here, we will die. If we go into the city, people are already eating their children there, so will we die of hunger. If we go to the camp of the Syrians, at least there could be food to eat and if they kill us, so be it. There is no point sitting to die like idle men. Let's take our destinies into our hands, who knows maybe something good may happen. That was a reasoned argument and intellectual situation analysis.

Off to the camp of the Syrians they headed…and the Lord of hosts stepped in. Their footsteps were magnified as that of a million horses and chariots. The Syrians heard the sound of their feet and fled in a hurry, abandoning their food, jewelry, ornaments, gold, silver etc. The spoil was too much. The lepers ate and gathered spoils until they got tired. Then they reasoned again, "It is not good for us to be here enjoying by ourselves while our people perish of hunger in the city; let's go and tell the king's house what we see".

Mr I-Too-Know was made the director at the city gate. To make sure the word of the prophet came to pass, he saw food for the first time in a very long time with his eyes, but before it would enter his mouth, the people trampled him underfoot and he died. He thought his political appointment certified him to talk anyhow in every matter. After all, it is a free society and everybody is entitled to his own opinion; what is wrong with that? His doubt notwithstanding, there was food again at the gates of Samaria according to the word of the prophet; the earth is the Lords.

CHAPTER 16

FREEDOM IN CAPTIVITY

Jehoakim reigned in Judah in the years when Nebuchadnezzar reigned in Babylon. In those days, the Babylonian kingdom was a world power...the throne of Nebuchadnezzar was so established that his words were laws that can neither be challenged nor revoked except as he pleased.

Everything seemed good in Judah under Jehoakim until his third year when Nebuchadnezzar besieged Judah and the Lord delivered her to him. He took everything he wanted, both people and the articles dedicated to God, and brought them into the treasure house of his gods. But he was neither godly nor god fearing and did whatsoever seemed right to him.

Some of the children of Israel who were taken into captivity were Daniel, Hananiah (Shedrack) Mishael (Meshach) and Azariah (Abed-Nego). These Hebrew youngmen had understanding of the times and the seasons. They could have lost faith in God for delivering their land into the hands of an ungodly nation, but they chose to be faithful. When everybody else was sitting down, they stood up to stand out of the crowd. They chose to identify with God even when it was unpopular. Those who know their God will always be strong, and they do exploits. But standing up for God in Babylon was neither safe nor smart, by the thinking of the day. It was a very politically incorrect thing to do. If God was any good, why did an ungodly nation conquer His people? Makes sense, right?

Nebuchadnezzar woke up one day and decided to select the best of the young men in the land to prepare them for his service. These were some of the children of Israel, some of the King's descendants and some of the nobles (Dan.1:3)…young men in whom there was no blemish. They were good looking, gifted in all wisdom, possessing knowledge and quick to understand; who had ability to serve in the king's palace, and whom they might teach the language and literature of the Chaldeans (Dan.1:4). Excellence is the watch word because nothing but the choicest belongs to the king, who was ready to invest in them. An aptitude test was conducted before enlistment.

The king knew that the way to get these young men acculturated in the kingdom was to teach them the language and literature of the Chaldeans. To serve the king, they needed to be able to communicate with him and the royal family, and to understand the culture of royalty. He appointed daily provisions for them and set Ashpenaz over them.

Although they were good looking, he wanted them to look refreshed and be their best. With the delicacies that are available only for the king and his nobles, he catered for them. They were to eat his food and drink his wine for three years.

But Daniel proposed in his heart that he would not defile himself with the king's food. How is eating the king's food defilement? When we became Christians, we had the zeal of the Lord...so much that we fasted and prayed as if there was no tomorrow. We looked at food as if it would defile us especially when we had to attend fellowship meetings. It was not acceptable for anybody to decorate tables for us with food in a manner that suggested eating the food before we actually ended our fast. Our anchor scripture then was "Man shall not live by bread alone".

Some of us went to solitary places to tarry for upwards of ten days fasting and praying, seeking the face of God on a number of issues of interest and/or concern. Others just fasted to put the flesh under control, or to live a more godly life. How good it is to live life, without being a slave, even to food.

There are people who are addicted to food so much that they cannot skip a meal and still function normally. There are several Christians reading this book, who cannot remember the last time they fasted, even ordinary skipping the breakfast. Unfortunately, we still turn around and wonder why we are so powerless in a generation where unrighteousness multiplies exponentially. Food is good, but you don't want to be enslaved to it.

Daniel knew he could not win the game by playing by their rules. By refusing to eat the king's delicacies, he demonstrated that he was in Babylon but not of Babylon. How would you eat what they eat and not think like they think and do like they do? Daniel was different, but was not ashamed to be. He was glad to stand alone than to stand with people who are not moved by the things that move him, or who are moved by the things that don't move him. He chooses vegetables instead.

In such a short period of ten days, the difference was already clear. Every time you decide to stand up for God, He will cause men to stand up for you. The decision not to defile himself was not to promote himself but to promote God. In taking a stance, he demonstrates that man shall not look good and fresh by eating the king's delicacies, but by the hand of God upon his life. By that singular stance, Daniel begins to challenge the prevalent thinking of the Chaldeans, but by humble submission, not by outright rebellion.

One of the ways to win a battle is to fight from a realm with which you are familiar. If you play by their rules, they will ruin you. God did not grow Adam and Eve by feeding them with bread. Even when that was necessary, he fed the Israelites with manna and quail. Elijah also, was he not fed by the raven at Brook Cherith? Who told Nebuchadnezzar that his delicacy is more delicious than God's delicacy? Whose delicacy would you choose: the king's or the king of king's? Daniel chooses the later. "Take my yoke upon you, for my yoke is easy and my burden is light".

One person's delicacy is another person's taboo. You don't understand this until you have traveled to different parts of the world or privileged to have lived or worked with people from different parts of the world. Culture is it! It is simply the way we do things and the things we value.

It was the culture of the Hebrew boys to submit to authorities. They submitted to the king's orders and learnt the culture and literature of the Chaldeans. The way to freedom is through the path of obedience. God gave Daniel favor and goodwill in the sight of the chief of the eunuchs. Again, favor can take a man farther than labor will take him. That is the reason the chief listened to Daniel in the first place, and granted his request. God blessed the veggies and water because His name was at stake.

Moreover, Daniel made a deal with the chief to test this proposal for just ten days and if it didn't work, to do whatsoever he wanted to do. It was a secret deal between them. It is only fools that challenge proofs. When the chief had seen the result for himself, the portion of their delicacy was taken away, and veggies were served. It was the first time that the king's orders were thwarted without any repercussions. Why? The approach.

God decorated the Hebrew boys with knowledge and skill in all literature and wisdom; and Daniel had understanding in all visions and dreams. By the time their training was over, the king performed another aptitude test, this time comparing with the magicians and the astrologers within the domain of his regime, and none was to be compared with the four Hebrew boys. They were selected to serve the king. What an honor for slaves to be preferred over and above the nobles.

CHAPTER 17

ALL THINGS WORK TOGETHER

THE UNCOMMON DEMAND: NEBUCHADNEZZAR DREAMS (Dan 2:1ff)

There are many theological and philosophical arguments on the subject of dreams. What are dreams? How do they come about? How do you verify the authenticity of dreams? What if you forget? Can you reverse your dreams by prayers? Why do you remember some dreams and forget others? What is the place of spirituality in dreams and the dream world? Is every dream from God? These are some of the questions people have asked about dreams.

It is not uncommon for people to dream dreams and then forget what it was all about. Every one of us has had such an experience. Sometime all you remember is that you had a dream last night. In some occasions, you are actually worried about it even though most people take it as normal..."they are only dreams, and dreams are not real". In different cultures they have different ways of treating dreams; some take them seriously, others don't.

Even Christians differ in their approaches to dreams. There are different theories out there about how dreams come about. While we don't intend to push for any doctrines of dreams in this book, we believe that God still speaks to people through the instrumentality of dreams. Other people claim their dreams manifest in the opposite, but I believe it depends on your spiritual maturity and the grace/gifts of God upon your life. "The old ones shall dream dreams…"

People have come to a point in their spiritual maturity where they actually demand a replay of their dreams or a continuation of a dream that was interrupted. God is able to do what he wants to do, even in the dream world.

What is strange and uncommon about King Nebu's dream is not the source or the content, rather it is the fact that he insisted that somebody else must tell him the dream and its interpretation. Nobody expects such an "unreasonable" demand from their king. But it was God orchestrating promotion for Daniel and his Hebrew brethren. Ironically, God had not aforetime revealed His plans to anybody on this issue. Also, it had not been heard in the land that any king requested such a difficult thing from anybody.

Freedom, just like promotion comes by solving difficult problems. The dream that troubled the king so much that he could not sleep was a serious national challenge. He had thought that no problem would defy the expertise of his magicians, astrologers, sorcerers and the Chaldeans. He had them in their multitudes, oblivious of the fact that a king is not saved by the multitude of his "wise men". As knowledgeable as they were, the secret things belong to God and He reveals them to whomsoever He wills. It is therefore little wonder that the kings' trusted professionals failed him in the day of adversity.

Knowledge is good, wisdom is desirable but it is the fear of God that harnesses these to solve problems that will endure the test of time. The secrets of God are for those that fear Him, not for sorcerers. Unless the Lord sets a man free, in vain is the prison gate open to his own eyes. Have you wondered why people who go to jail for one offence are likely going to be repeat offenders unless the Lord touches and changes them?

Even though the Hebrew boys were found to be ten times more ready to serve the king they were still slaves. Although the nobles envied them, yet they had no freedom like the nobles. Every teaching they received was to make them more Babylonian ... an idol worshipping nation. They had to excel in the language, culture and literature of the Babylonians to enable them acclimatize to the lifestyle even at the palace.

When the wise men of Babylon could not meet the kings' demand, an urgent decree was made to kill all of them. Oh yes, it would have been their pleasure to start with Daniel and the Hebrew boys. That is the lot of slaves everywhere. In those days, if the oracles requested a human head for lunch, it was the head of a slave that was willingly offered. The chief priest could wake up one day and say that the bad omen in the land is because the gods are hungry of human sacrifice, however many slaves he requested, those would be offered, no questions asked.

So Daniel and his colleagues knew it was a matter of life and death as it was for the wise men of Babylon. Are you surprised that foreigners are the first to be retrenched long before a company goes under? But those who know their God are always strong, doing exploits. Daniel knew that the secrets of God are available through revelation to those who love Him. He knew what to do and how to do it. He therefore requested of the king "time".

THE IMPORT OF TIME

Time is very important to everybody. If you can invest time to any pursuit, impossibilities can become possible, mountains can move, and power can change hands. Time is a mover that moves things and brings about change. If you have faith and keep knocking at the door, time will justify the effort you put in place.

Persistence is a function of time. Rugged faith is an accomplice of time. The dream career you want is a product of time, so is your freedom from every oppression, suppression, manipulation and the like, be it in the community, church or the marketplace.

Why would the righteous perish with the unrighteous? God is a faithful judge and a covenant keeper. He would spare the righteous and glorify His name especially when the righteous stands for his faithfulness in God, regardless. In time, He revealed the secret to Daniel. Nobody could believe it, not even the king.

That revelation saved the Hebrew boys and the Chaldeans from untimely death, and of course the Hebrew boys also moved from slavery to relative freedom, and promotion in the kingdom. For the sake of a handful righteous people, God could save a whole nation from disaster. How wonderful it is that the creator of the universe cares for us, and expects us to maintain a relationship with him.

ARIOCH CLAIMS THE GLORY

As the matter was made known to Daniel, he appeared before Arioch to request audience with the king so as to make known to him the dream and its interpretation. "I have found a man of the captives of Judah that will tell you the interpretation of the dream". You did not find him, he came to you. Arioch was the boss, yet he couldn't interpret the dream. Now he wants credit for it. He wants the king to see him as diligently doing a great job. How can the monkey be working, and the baboon will be eating? Is that fair?

People like Arioch don't go far in life and ministry. Those are people who seek self promotion, self-recognition and self-domination. They live in bondage of those self issues. Did you hear anything else about Arioch in the rest of the story? You probably never really knew who he was until now.

Now contrast Arioch with Daniel. Daniel did not claim any glory from the revelation. He gave glory to God. "As for me, this secret is not revealed to me for any wisdom that I have more than any living, but for their sakes". Although it guaranteed deliverance from the hasty decree of the king, the righteous as well as the unrighteous benefitted from the freedom orchestrated by the revelation and subsequent interpretation of the dream. He assures the king that the dream is certain and the interpretation sure. That indicates that there are dreams that are improbable, or even outright uncertain.

What did the king himself do? He fell down and worshipped Daniel and promoted him. Daniel became great, and was appointed to a rulership position as chief of the governors over all the wise men of Babylon. At his request, his brethren that prayed with him were all promoted and set over the affairs of the provinces of Babylon.

As for Daniel, he sat at the gate of the king. Do you know what he was doing? To administer judgment in the kingdom and to direct the activities of the so-called wise men. That is something that could be akin to a chief of staff at the palace. That is a secular position. It had not been known that a Hebrew slave could occupy such a position in a pagan nation. Do you think the wise men were happy about it?

THE GOLDEN IMAGE: THE FIERY FURNACE

Again we see what time can do: it makes people forget things or change behavior. Was it not King Nebuchadnezzar who fell down and worshipped Daniel in acknowledgement that the God of Daniel is the only true God? Now we are told he made a golden image. It was the dedication party and all the nobles of the land were gathered.

Then it was commanded that everybody must worship the golden image at the sound of the trumpet. The initiators of that commandment knew that Daniel and the Hebrew boys would not obey that ungodly decree. Those were men who stood up for God in the most dangerous situations, and lived lives of freedom in a situation of bondage; and pleased God rather than men. For them, to live is for God and to die living for God, is gain.

There is no wonder that the Chaldeans spied on them and brought accusations to the king that there was disobedience in the land. They were accused of mutiny- insubordination to the king. They would not bulge until the king executed their wish on the offenders. In fact, they accused the king of setting the Hebrew boys over the affairs of the province…a statement that amply demonstrates their dissatisfaction with the king's decisions. "There are certain Jews whom you have set over the affairs of the province of Babylon –Shedrach, Meshach and Abednego- these men have not regarded you: they serve not your gods nor worship the golden image". They knew about Daniel and his position in the kingdom, but thought they could mess with the other three Jews. Apparently, they were not bold to accuse Daniel, probably to stay out of trouble. It was time for the other three to defend their faith in God, and they did just fine.

The king verified the accusation and would have given the Jews yet a second chance to run away from the punishment "...and who is that God that shall deliver you out of my hands?" They heard him clearly and did understand the battle line but were not careful to answer him in that matter.

We are not going to join issues with you and your men. We do not have to wait until we hear the sound of the trumpet to let you know our position. Our God whom we serve is able to deliver us from the furnace and He will deliver us out of your hand (Dan. 3:17). However, if God chooses not to deliver us, be it known to you oh king that we will not serve your gods nor worship your golden image. Go right ahead and do what you want to do. There is no shifting ground here. We are not going to be politically correct, neither do we need to think twice about it. The battle line was drawn – the price for freedom. This is freedom of speech exemplified.

Little wonder the king's anger was furious and his visage changed. His commandment was urgent. At his commandment, the furnace was made seven times hotter.

The strongest of his army picked up the Hebrew boys, bound them and cast them into the furnace, but the flame of the furnace grazed the men that threw the Hebrew boys to it. Hence the strongest of his soldiers died in an attempt to execute the king's urgent commandment. That is the reward for refusing to heed the injunction "touch not mine anointed and do my prophets no harm".

"Did we not bind and cast three men into the fire?" I see four men loose, and walking in the midst of the fire, and they have no hurt, and the form of the fourth is like the son of God. How did he know that? The king tremblingly beckoned on them to come out, calling them "servants of the Most High God". The golden image may have been a high god to the king, but he testified by his own mouth that the God of Shedrach, Meshach and Abednego is the Most High God. He was and still is the most high. Ultimate freedom, undoubtedly dwells with the Most High God.

The accusers and spies that reported the Hebrew boys witnessed it live; so did the governors, captains, counselors: that the fire had no power whatsoever over the Hebrew boys – their clothes, hairs, skin etc were untouched. Not even the smell of fire or smoke was on them. It was the strangest thing the Babylonians witnessed till that day. Obviously, they were up against a stronger power, and nobody could challenge the evidence. The families of the strongest and over-zealous soldiers witnessed their husbands, fathers, sons, in-laws and friends as they were grazed by the flame of the fire. What a contrast!

King Nebuchadnezzar blessed the God of Shedrach, Meshach, and Abednego for delivering His servants who changed the king's words by choosing to die rather than obey ungodly injunctions. The king decreed again that nobody should speak against the God of Shedrach, Meshach, and Abednego; otherwise the persons would be cut in pieces and their houses shall be made a dunghill: "for there is no other God that can deliver after this sort". The Babylonians were not happy that at the request of Daniel, Shedrack, Meshach and Abednego were appointed to positions. That was why they spied and reported them to the king. Now on his own accord, the king promoted them. Promotion comes, neither from the east nor west.

THE DREAM BE TO THEM THAT HATE YOU

"Let my counsel be acceptable unto you and break off thy sins by righteousness and thine iniquities by showing mercy to the poor" (Vs 19). One year passed by and the king still did not change. He did not take the dream and its interpretation seriously. He did not escape from the wrath of God, and pride was still in him. Pride does not secure or guarantee freedom, it leads only to bondage. It does not lift a man up, it weighs him down. It does not secure a throne, it dethrones a man.

"Is not this great Babylon that I have built for the house of the kingdom by the might of my power, and for the honor of my majesty"? Do you see boasting in arrogance and pride? I, my, mine ...As he yet spoke, the kingdom was taken from him. He was driven from men, and dwelt with beasts and grazed with the oxen. At the end of seven years his senses returned. His throne returned, his nobles came back to him, his kingdom was re-established, he confessed that there is none like Jehovah and none can stay His hand or say to him "what doest thou"? He concluded that the ways of God are judgment and those who work in pride He is able to abase.

Freedom does not come by romancing with any government in power. It is not obtained by being politically correct neither is it by obeying every commandment, howbeit ungodly. When faced with two options, one has to choose whose slave he has to be, or who calls the shots in his life. Freedom has to happen inside of you before it happens around you...it is a waste of energy to look for freedom outside when one is still a slave inside. Only time separates one from external freedom when internal and eternal freedom have been secured.

Compromise does not guarantee freedom, it actually guarantees slavery. Fear of men and the power of the king keeps one a slave. The laws of the Chaldeans are not revocable, but several times we have seen it compromised because the Hebrew boys would not worship any other

God but Jehovah. When the people plotted disgrace and demotion, even death by the fiery furnace, God turned it around, not just to glorify Himself but to promote them. How can you beat that?

Taking the Jews captive is one thing, taking the sacred things in the house of God is another yet desecrating the sacred things is a much serious abomination. If you are a slave master, you can mess around with slaves but you must be careful what you do with their God. The Jews did not fail in serving the Babylonian kingdom, having learnt the culture and language. They excelled both in the administration and service of the king, but they would not stop at anything that wanted to interfere with their relationship with God.

Some brethren who were fervent in their service to God become lukewarm once they get married, get a new job, have a baby etc. Most times we let the issues, cares and worries of life get in the way of our relationship with God. When things go wrong, or we are sick, that is enough reason to let the service of God or our commitment to him wait for a while. Likewise, when we get our dream job, then we can as well excuse God for a while so we can get going on the new job. Other people get so mad, maybe when a loved one passes away, that they let the grief come in the way of their devotion, worship and service to God; not the Hebrew boys that the Book of Daniel tells us about.

THE FINGER WRITING ON THE WALL

Belshazzar took over the reign of the land after his father Nebuchadnezzar. Did he not grow up in the palace? How is it that he didn't seem to know about Daniel? Was he so royalty minded that the Hebrew slaves meant little or nothing to him? After all they were mere slaves. If they were so good and smart, why couldn't they defend their land and themselves when Nebuchadnezzar overtook them and brought them as slaves?

His kingdom was so great he had over a thousand lords who attended the great wine drinking party. He was king, so could do whatever he wanted in his kingdom. The seven years of his father's abasement did not teach him lessons. The silver vessels which his father had taken out of the temple in Jerusalem were the best cups in the land for his feast? So his concubines, wives, and princes desecrated the Lord's vessels in arrogance.

"As they drank, they praised the gods of gold, and silver, of brass, of iron, and of stone" (Dan.5:4). They did not know the battle line they just drew…apparently they mocked God and praised their god for delivering the silver wares from the temple of Jehovah to their hands, even for such occasions as wine party. They obviously overstepped their boundaries and God would not let them go scot-free.

That same hour came forth a finger of a man's hand and wrote upon the wall of the king's palace and the king saw the part of the hand that wrote. His countenance changed, his thoughts were troubled, the joints of his loins were loosed and his knees smote against each other. Despite his offer for a handsome reward, the astrologers, Chaldeans, soothsayers, wise men of Babylon and all the ambitious people of the land could not read or interpret the handwriting on the wall. He thought he was in charge of the land of Babylon and was going to appoint a third ruler in the land, not knowing that his regime was over. There was fire on the mountain. The earth is indeed the Lords and the fullness thereof.

Is it not the duty of queens to bring glad tidings at a time of distress so the countenance of the king would not change? So did she. "Let not your countenance be changed; there is a man in the kingdom in whom the spirit of the holy gods dwells, and in the days of your father, light and understanding and wisdom, like the wisdom of the gods, was found in him". Where was Belshazzar all these years? So she remembered the exploit of Daniel yet they did not seek the God of Daniel? In any case, she counseled him to bring Daniel in and the riddle would be solved.

Daniel was a Spirit man, but he did not use his gifting to oppress his oppressors. "Are you that Daniel of the children of the captivity of Judah, whom my father the king brought out of Jerusalem? This is ridiculous. Belshazzar was so kingly, yet so ignorant. Arrogance dwelt so much in him. He spoke like he just came down from the moon the night before.

Daniel did not need any of his scarlet clothes, gold chains or rulership appointments. Daniel knew better than that. He was neither interested in all those, nor did he ever want to identify with the ungodly successor of an ungodly king that would not learn from past experiences. "Your gifts be to yourself". You probably need the gifts you are promising more than anybody else.

Daniel appeared to have said "let me refresh your memory of things you know about. It was the Most High God that gave your father the kingdom, majesty, glory and honor. Everything your father did came from what he was given – majesty. When his heart was lifted up, and his mind hardened in pride, he was deposed from his kingly throne and his glory departed. For seven years, he dwelt among beasts and ate grass until he knew that the earth is the Lord's".

"You knew all these things that happened to your father yet you did not humble your heart; instead you lifted up yourself against the Lord of heaven and drank wine with the sacred vessels from the temple of God with your lords, nobles, wives, and concubines. You even broke the first commandment by praising gods of all kinds of things that do not see or hear but the one that gave you life and the throne have you not glorified. Now you have landed yourself in trouble. Your cup is full, you have been judged and the jury is out. God cannot stand one more day of your arrogance".

- God has numbered your kingdom and finished it
- You have been weighed on a balance and found wanting
- Your kingdom has been divided and given to the Medes and Persians

That same night, he was slain and Darius the Median took the kingdom.

HANGING OUT WITH HUNGRY LIONS

Daniel was set over the presidents whom Darius set over the affairs of the land. Again, the nobles, princes, governors and presidents were not happy a slave was set over them, so they sought occasion to get him into trouble by all means. But those who know their God shall be strong, in fact, they do exploits.

While they could not find any occasion against Daniel, they knew it was going to be through his God. So they gathered, and plotted evil, and got the king to make it a law in the land and to seal it with his signet ring so that it can neither be changed nor be voided according to the laws of the Medes and Persians. It did not occur to the king that this was a devilish ploy to waste Daniel. No man is killed unless the God of heaven has allowed it.

A statue was made, a decree followed and anybody who refuses to worship it for 30 days would be thrown into the den of lions. When Daniel heard it, he went home, knelt down before his God as his manner was, and worshipped his God three times a day. As was expected, the people spied him out and reported to the king insisting that the law of Media and Persia changes not. The king would have delivered Daniel, but he could not prevail over the accusers so he obliged them but prayed that the Lord God of Daniel would deliver him.

Anytime you are successful in a foreign land, you have to constantly watch over your shoulders. The nobles were jealous, and they did not care about the impact of their jealousy on the government of the day. The king knew that he needed Daniel for a smooth running of the daily business of the kingdom so he did not want to lose him. That is freedom, even in the land of captivity.

Daniel was thrown into the den of lions, but he played with hungry lions all night long as the lion of the tribe of Judah shut up the mouth of those lions. The lions probably saw Daniel like one of them. The son of a lion is a lion. In fact, the presence of Daniel in the den was apparently the most awesome experience the lions have ever had.

They played with him, probably their hunger pangs seized, even though they were hungry. His presence probably affected their body biochemistry. This is operating in the super natural. When we serve God, He takes care of our business and safety. A man is not saved by connecting to the king...even Darius went home and fasted as he prayed for Daniel; it was beyond his power.

The next morning, he did not even wash his face or brush his mouth before he ran to the den to check on Daniel, who was surprisingly intact and talking. The king happily brought him out and in his stead, the accusers and their families were cast into the den to make feast for the lions…not even their bones were left uncrushed. How great is the Lord! Freedom lies with him.

The law of the land is changed again. The God of Daniel is proclaimed the only true God because no other god delivers after this manner. A decree went forth commanding all to worship the God of Daniel. By his refusal to obey ungodly rules and commandments, Daniel has again preached the gospel and changed the direction of things all over the kingdoms and regions of over three kings.

CHAPTER 18

FRUITS WORTHY OF FREEDOM

As in most of Bible stories, Vashti represents a person, as it does a character. She was born in a lineage of royalty and became the queen in the days of Ahasuerus partly by serendipity. Although familiar with the royal lifestyle, it was King Ahasuerus that made her queen, by choice. She must have exercised so much power and authority in the kingdom, but those were delegated powers. When a man appoints you to a position, he can disappoint you from it. That is why people who have understanding hold unto God for their promotions.

No man would promote you higher than himself unless if by law and policy, he is disqualified for the position. Even then, he would still want to be the god-father....let you be in the office, and he would be in power. Have you not seen such arrangements? If you dare disobey your god-father, he would fight you with everything he has, and if it be possible, disgrace you from office.

Political freedom readily comes to mind anytime the subject of freedom is discussed. I do not play partisan politics, even though I am of the opinion that man is a political animal. However, I know, but do not quite approve of the fact that politicians determine the fate of the rest of us, regardless of our specialty, endeavor or accolades. That probably explains why many people need freedom from the love of political power, especially those who believe they were born to rule.

Vashti was a very influential personality. She had, at her reach and disposal, all the instruments of governance. She could make laws and enact decrees but only by remaining submissive to the authority of her husband, the king. For purposes of clarity, let us recall that she was the great-granddaughter of King Nebuchadnezzar of Babylon and the daughter of King Belshazzar. In the days of Belshazzar her father, it is claimed that a mob from Medes and Persians attacked, murdered Belshazzar and kidnapped his daughter, courtesy of the great King Darius of Persia.

Apparently because of her beauty, King Darius took pity on her and gave her to his son Ahasuerus to marry. Other than that, she should have been a slave girl in that kingdom. By her promotion to the position of queen, rather than just one of the numerous wives or concubines, she had access to the instruments of rulership, and soon began to wield influence in the land, over and above every other woman. I do not think that she forgot how far she came to be. Not so much is known, with certainty, about her and her lifestyle until the banquet that preceded her demotion and ultimately, banishment.

When the king made a feast for his nobles, she also made her own feast for the women. Historians and biblical scholars have different interpretations for the concurrent hosting events in the land. She had known the king so well that she could complete his sentences. Can you imagine the honor she had among women and the nobles of the land?

Some women liberation enthusiasts make references to Vashti as the first woman to demand her rights or exercise her freedom to do what she believes to be right. When the king requested her to come and showcase her beauty for his nobles, she refused. She probably considered that the king was drunk and she probably thought he wouldn't mind as always. In the contrary, it was not business as usual.

While we do not intend to argue for or against the king's request, we intend to look at Vashti's response through the freedom prism. It does seem that Vashti is an independent minded modern day queen that lived then. Unfortunately, it was not her kingdom, but his; and a ship is not controlled by two captains at the same time. Today, people hide under the freedom mentality to do what pleases them and what they please, and nobody should bother them.

King Ahasuerus may not have demoted Vashti for her disregard of his commands if not for the counsel of Memucan, one of the seven princes of Persia and Media who saw the king's face, sat first in the kingdom, wise men who knew the times. As soon as the king summoned the wise men, he asked them what should be done to Vashti according to law for refusing to do the King's bidding.

"Vashti has not done wrong to the king only, but also to the princes, and to all the peoples that are in all the provinces of the King", about one hundred and twenty seven provinces that span from India unto Ethiopia. The wise men interpreted Vashti's refusal (in their drunken state) from a national perspective, taking into consideration the alleged multiplier effects and encouragement for women in the kingdom to despise their husbands.

According to them, if the king ignored that action, it was going to lead to much contempt and wrath in the kingdom when women make references to it. Memucan's suggestion was then very much received by these "drunk" men. The laws of Media and Persia do not change, once it is sealed with the king's signet ring.

"Let go forth a royal commandment, and let it be written among the laws that it will not be altered. Let Vashti come no more before King Ahasuerus; and let her royal estate be given to somebody who is better than she". It pleased the king to take a permanent decision when he was temporarily upset. Can you see any wisdom in that? Oh, lest I forget…he only exercised his kingly freedom.

Beauty is a good servant, but can be a bad master. Everybody is created beautiful, but society decides that some people are more beautiful than others, but that does not mean that individuals who refuse to succumb to societal standards and popular opinions, do not have their personal preferences. So Vashti was beautiful, but when Esther showed up, the people knew that the beautiful ones are not yet born.

Some people have messed up their lives because it got into their heads that everybody admires their beauty. Physical beauty is good, but highly insufficient to lead anybody to a lasting state of freedom. People may be attracted to you by reason of your beauty, but that is not enough to keep them. Sometime, you hear the elders describe somebody as good outside, bad inside. That is a big minus. In fact, many people out there are not married because they are good outside, bad inside. Even in a generation where divorce is on the increase…many beautiful and handsome people are divorced several times because they are not as good inside as they are outside. Could that be the situation with Vashti?

The king of Media and Persia did not have to negotiate with anybody in any of his provinces. He makes laws to suit his occasions and feelings. All he needs do is append his signet ring. Vashti knew this, but did she let royalty get in the way of her loyalty? What else could she do for the king if not to make him happy? How free is an ex-captive who became first lady? It probably took one single disobedience and she was out. God gives us second chances but with man, it could be a different ball game.

It is also possible that she has always disobeyed the king and got away with it. However, the setting of this event and the interpretation given to it meant that Vashti overestimated her chances and over-stepped her bounds.

The king could have ordered her beheaded. He could have done to her whatever seemed good to him, but we are not told anything else about her. As far as I am concerned, she stopped existing in the affairs of the kingdom. She woke up that day a queen, and went to bed that night a cast-away. It was a very expensive mistake – the kind we discussed in "Unguarded Moments".

Vashti as a model: Another Perspective

The book of Esther and the themes that emerge from it have been interpreted in a way to give credit to Esther. Several people have named their children after her, and not many of us have seen people named after Vashti. But I believe that Vashti was not as bad as she is presented. In many quarters, she is viewed as an over ambitious wife of a king who did not know her boundaries.

Why did Vashti refuse to do the king's bidding? This question has not been answered conclusively, leaving people to make speculations. While some people believe she wanted to disrespect the king in the public, it is probably unlikely that a queen who is not drunk would want to do that. Other people believe she let her beauty get into her head, so she thought she could use it to advance herself and do what she pleases, but that actually appears to be what Esther did under Mordecai's directives.

While lots of people think Esther is a heroine, others actually believe that Vashti deserves that honor. She comes across to her fans as a woman of character, who should have a good understanding of consequences of her action, yet did not compromise her standards. While it is not clear how the king wanted her to appear before his drunk guests, it does seem that she was supposed to appear wearing only her royal crown.

That means appearing before the men in total or partial nudity. Is that not what women do in our generation as a way to attract the attention of men? Prevalent mentality is that a dress is not sexy unless it exposes some part of the woman's body, especially the parts that are supposed to be covered. How many women in the churches today wear such body-exposing dresses even to church events? If a pagan queen would risk a throne because of her refusal to appear "exposed" before men, and considered her dignity of more importance than the throne, then what are we talking about?

I think Vashti knew the difference between royalty and loyalty. Even though Esther was chosen for the king as a replacement, the king remembered Vashti and what was done to her, after the effect of the wine was gone. Does that not imply that he regretted what he did to her? Do you make a permanent decision because you are temporarily upset?

It is only in unguarded moments that people do things that way. Even the counselors were not good counselors…they were also drunk. Alcohol has a way of turning wisdom into foolishness. These were known to be wise men, but they took a rash decision in their drunken state.

I understand that we see it from the perspective that it was God at work setting up the stage for the deliverance of Israel, however what was done to Vashti is not commendable. Her refusal to appear before the "drunk" men was blown out of proportion. She did not mean to disrespect all the men in the kingdom, nor did she do anything that conclusively suggests she wanted to give the women ideas. She just fell on the wrong side of history on that day.

Although we are not told about how she actually became queen, we have an idea about the processes involved when Esther was chosen. She must have been the choice lady in her own time, and even the day of her debasement the king still acknowledged that she was a beauty to behold.

After she was exiled, no mention of her was made again. It would be good to know that she probably became free from all the issues involved in being the queen, in a pagan kingdom, where the king and his household are ready targets for coups and attacks from both internal and external aggressors. She probably had a better life as an ex-queen than as a queen. Today, she would probably win a Nobel Prize for refusing to expose her body when everybody else thought if it came from the king, it must be obeyed. I hope Mordecai did not think so as well, otherwise why did he refuse to bow down to Haman in obedience to the king's orders?

MORDECAI, THE GATE MASTER

There is a place for positioning and location in the affairs and business of life. In the book of Daniel, we see that King Nebuchadnezzar took certain Jews captive in the days of Jeconiah king of Judah. A Benjamite, Mordecai raised Esther, his uncle's daughter after her parents passed away. So he doubled as Esther's uncle and step-father. He played the roles of a guardian, director, manager etc in the plot of deliverance that would ultimately come to the Jews.

The demotion and dismissal of Vashti created a vacancy in the kingdom for the office of a queen. Esther probably never thought, nor could she have imagined herself becoming queen in this pagan kingdom. However, Mordecai believed that she had a chance. He instructed her on what to do and to conduct herself. It all worked out fine.

Of particular interest in the life of Esther is that we see favor in action. Where labor stops, favor starts. Mordecai could not have succeeded if Esther did not find favor, both with the keeper of women and the king. However, it was politically essential that her proper identity was not known so as not to bias the selection process. If they had known she was a Jew, chances are that they would have discriminated against her. Mordecai knew this very well. He would not rest, but walked before the court of the women's house everyday to know how Esther did, and what would become of her.

When it was the turn of Esther to go and see the king, she requested nothing but what the keeper appointed. All she needed was favor, which does not always respond to beauty, intelligence, age, height, size etc. The race is not always to the swift. When the hand of God is upon a person, or thing, speed comes, promotion comes, increase comes, freedom comes.

As soon as the king saw Esther he loved her above all the virgins, so he set the royal crown upon her head and made her queen instead of Vashti. That was a very improbable promotion, to a position of influence and authority. Mordecai knew it was all for good. He knew the importance of political power in a land of captivity.

Believe it or not, Mordecai knew the powers that Esther had more than Esther herself knew it. She was naïve and never aspired to this position – she did not qualify for it. Even if it was to be voted, who would vote for a little orphan slave girl? Even if she was a citizen, she was at best a second class citizen. The events that brought her to power were improbable, but obviously there was a hand that worked things out behind the scene.

Ostensibly, Vashti refused to respond to the king because her days were over. She was demoted so Esther would step into power. Esther came into power so the Jews would be delivered. It may not really have been Vashti's fault that these series of events happened because she refused to respond to the demands of her king. It may be that the prayers of the Jews had gotten to God, and the day of deliverance was around the corner.

Because Esther was now in the palace, Mordecai sat at the king's gate. Apparently, the people did not link her to this Jew because she had not made her identity known, not even to the king. He became a self-appointed secret service agent to the king. When Bigthan and Teresh, the kings chamberlains plotted coup against the king, he heard it and made it known to Esther who then informed the king.

When the matter was investigated, it was found to be nothing but the truth. Without delay, the full weight of the law prevailed over the chamberlains and it was documented in the book of the chronicles of the king. Again God was orchestrating deliverance, and freedom for the Jews through this ordinary but apparently ambitious Mordecai.

When the king ordered to kill Haman, he did not summon any meeting but to demote Vashti, he sought counsel with the wise men. When he selected Esther as queen he didn't ask any wise man for opinions, but when he wanted to honor Mordecai he asked Haman of his opinion. The king didn't, and didn't have to act in a certain way. However, it is remarkable that Esther and Mordecai were not any kind of special people, only that they were at the right side of history in their generation. If anything, Mordecai was a hypocrite, and maintained a double standard. I am not even sure he had a job, otherwise why would he sit at the king's gate all the time, and walk up and down the court all day to see how Esther faired? Did he have something else to do? Did he have a family? What was his career?

Was he ambitious of political position or did he hear from God to push Esther to compete for the office of the queen? We may not have all the details of what happened when the Virgins took their turns to spend a night with the king in his selection process, but Mordecai was ok with it. He wanted to use Esther's beauty to advance himself in the kingdom, and he did. He must have bowed down to the king, and people bowed down to him after he was promoted by the same king who promoted Haman, a man he refused to bow down to, claiming he was a Jew. What a double standard! While it is ok to credit him with the deliverance of the Jews, it will also be argued that he caused their ordeals as well. Was he a better Jew than anybody else? Why did he have to attach civil disobedience to the Jewish nation?

He thought that being a Jew was enough excuse to pick and choose which instructions to obey and which ones to ignore. He arrogated more freedom to himself than he actually had. He didn't honor Haman yet he didn't refuse the honor when it came to him. By all means, it seems he set out from the onset to get into the business of the palace, which eventually worked out by all means. I see Mordecai as somewhat an obnoxious politician, and it is understandable that Haman would be upset by mere sight of him. If they knew he was related to the queen, it would have been a different ball game.

The fact that he forbade Esther from disclosing her identity even to the king was very deceptive, and such a dangerous maneuver. As far as the king was concerned, Esther was one of the daughters of his kingdom. Even the people that work for the king at the gate or with the women did not know her true identity. That is high level fraud.

So Mordecai was a treacherous politician, and controlled Esther by manipulations. "If you do not do anything, salvation will come to the Jews and you and your household will not have any credits". Obviously he was motivated by profits, even if he had to risk the life of this little step-daughter. As a matter of principle, he sacrificed the life of Esther for his own benefit, when he made her appear before the king uninvited, and as long as she was queen with undisclosed identity.

Is that not what terrorists do? They sneak into your camp unidentified, and you think they are part of you. You trust them with your secrets, not knowing they are informants to the enemies. You wonder how and why your competitor carries out what you still plan to do just before your plans hatch. If you put your ears on the ground, you hear things that nobody else could have been able to know about you, your business or your family except an insider. Yet they do it so well, and are smart at it that you never would suspect them. That is Mordecai right there for you.

Even the queen was behaving like the small girl she was in Mordecai's house. She did not seem to have taken initiatives on her own. She was in office, Mordecai was in power.

The people at the gate discussed freely with Mordecai not knowing that everything they said got to the ears of the queen before the morrow. They didn't know an informant was in their midst. That is how they carelessly and freely shared their secret plan to overthrow the king, only to be overthrown because their plans were unfolded to the king before they were hatched. And they were hanged. Credit was given to Mordecai.

To get away from his bugging, Esther had to appear before the king uninvited "if I perish I perish". I do not think it was as much for the fact that she wanted to die for the Jews as it was that she wanted to get Mordecai off her back. It was an effort to please this obnoxious man who had to remind her how he took good care of her after her parents passed away. He apparently had to retell her how she owed him everything she had and had become.

Was Esther really ready to perish? I don't think so, otherwise why did she keep her identity a secret? Did she love and care for the king? I do not think so, after all It was Mordecai's idea. Was she even free to decide what she wanted? No way. Mordecai was over bearing, and the king was next to God in the land. Even when she invited the king and Haman to a dinner, she only played out a script that Mordecai had written for her.

She was not capable on her own, of summoning the king or even inviting him over for such an unsolicited request. It took her days of rehearsals, fasting and prayers to make that request. I give her credit for being able to do a good job at it, however I can imagine Mordecai making eye contacts with her, encouraging her to go ahead and make the request.

But Mordecai was a successful politician. The fact that we are talking about him now is credit to him. He achieved what he set out to achieve, because he got political appointments, supervised the killing, not just of his arch-enemy Haman, but the rest of the enemies of the Jews in the land. He was held in honor, and had voice in the affairs of the provinces of Medes and Persia.

MUCH ADO ABOUT FREEDOM: FINAL WORD

We have tried to understand freedom, first by discussing what it is not, using several examples and illustrations. We have also argued, from scriptures that man was not created to have absolute freedom in this life. First and foremost, if God wanted us to have unrestricted freedom, why did he plant the forbidden tree in the middle of the garden at Eden?

Secondly, why did he create man to know in part and to see in part? Why did he make us finite in our being and doing? In our knowledge, and understanding of life and the mysteries of death, God has kept the details far from the reach of our imagination. Can you explain that?

Great things have been achieved by men who are free to explore and to experiment; however freedom has also made man to doubt, challenge and question, even the existence of God. They cite different instances and theories to defend such positions. However, the more explanations they want to proffer, the more questions they raise.

One of the greatest gifts God gave us is the freedom and ability to discover ourselves. That is actually the greatest discovery there is to make, and the best thing man can do for himself. However, we have failed woefully in that respect. One area that amply illustrates that failure is our thinking that there is any such thing as absolute freedom. Make no mistakes about it. The more freedom you think you have, the more restricted and tethered you are.

For a Christian, and everybody else for that matter, there is freedom only in restrictions. Any effort made to gain freedom from censorship is an effort in futility. Even

Jesus did not have the kind of freedom we want. If he had it, why did he live a life of prayer? Why did he say "nevertheless, your will not mine be done"? Why did he pay taxes to Caesar? Why did he obey the laws of the land?

****

Christians have the power of choice. We exercise this power every time, whether it is to do good or bad. This freedom is available because we are no longer slaves to sin and the devil through the redemption power in the name of Jesus. Our captivity has been paid for so we are legally redeemed, and set free. That is ultimate freedom.

When Jesus said "It Is Finished", the deed was done. It was signed, sealed and delivered. It was total redemption. Even if you sin after that, you have an advocate with the father – the one who redeemed you from the legal hold of the devil. That sin does not make you a slave to sin, but an errant son, and your case is treated as such. The power of choice to live above sin is inside of you. When the prodigal son came back home, he was received.

An unsaved fellow is a slave to sin and the devil. He does not have the power to live above sin. The power to "become" helps us to "overcome". That difference might seem small, but it is very significant and far-reaching. For example, it is the power to become that sits us in the heavenly places, far above principalities and powers.

But with that freedom from sin and sinfulness comes a restriction and censorship in our thoughts, words and deeds as prescribed in scriptures.

The law of the Lord is perfect…refreshing the soul. It is in His law that we find freedom, it is also in it we find the restrictions that censor our thoughts and deeds. We are free only within the boundaries set by God. In fact, with its restrictions, the sphere of operation for a Christian within boundaries is greater and wider than any perceived freedom envisaged by the unsaved. This is because, within that boundary, our freedom is boundless. This is because within that boundary, we are actually Spirit beings.

This knowledge is refreshing and reassuring. It is echoed in Romans 8:2 "For the law of the Spirit of life in Christ Jesus has made me free from the law of sin and death". Also, in Gal. 5:1 it is clearly commanded "Stand fast therefore in the liberty wherewith Christ has made us free, and be not entangled again with the yoke of bondage".

There is liberty only where the Spirit of the Lord is (2 Cor.3:17). Therefore the only freedom worthy of your pursuit is freedom in Christ. Although it sounds like a contradiction, the only true freedom in Christ comes to those who are actually His slaves. But the slave of Christ is truly free. It may not win the vote of the day, but I dare tell you that only Christians have the Holy Spirit, therefore only Christians have liberty. However that freedom is often times abused. Hence, the essence of this book.

The name of the Lord is a strong tower, the righteous runs into it, and is safe.

I pray that the Lord will sanctify us with the truth in His Word. May His grace sustain us according to his purpose. I hope you will explore the freedom that is available in Christ. Today, if you hear His voice, harden not your heart. He seeks to set you free, and if the Son sets you free, you are free indeed.

Shalom!

Index

www.ingramcontent.com/pod-product-compliance
Lightning Source LLC
Chambersburg PA
CBHW032006060426
42449CB00032B/868
* 9 7 8 0 9 9 0 5 8 0 3 0 0 *